...ries ...ok,

Management Sta... ...as a

...eader and Manager, has bee... ...ateu ... ... Chinese, Arabic and

...eek and sold in the US, India, Australia and across Europe. Alan

...rks with individuals and with leaders to increase their

confidence, resilience, success and well-being. He formed Alan

Hester Associates in 2002, delivering practical, inspirational and

interactive workshops to a wide range of people. This book draws

on his experiences of working with people recovering from

depression and other mental health issues, long-term unemployed

adults, people with addiction problems and those who need help

to get out of their own way and find a new direction in life.

Alan lives with his wife Eunice, the couple's Golden Retriever and

their four cats in Reading, Berkshire. They have a son, Michael,

and a daughter, Charlotte. He spends his spare time listening to

Bob Dylan albums, supporting Reading FC, watching cricket,

gardening, reading and, of course, writing. *Get Out Of Your Own

Way* is his second book.

To find out more about the author's work or to contact him direct

for speaking, training or coaching, please visit www.alanhester.

o.uk or email him at alan@alanhester.co.uk.

Other Titles

Management Starts With You

Get Out Of Your Own Way

Alan Hester

A HOW TO BOOK

ROBINSON

ROBINSON

First published in Great Britain in 2018
by Robinson

10 9 8 7 6 5 4 3 2 1

A CIP catalogue record for this book
is available from the British Library.

Author's note
The names of individuals mentioned in
this book have been changed to protect
their privacy.

ISBN: 978-1-47214-037-1

Typeset in Sentinel Light by Hewer Text
UK Ltd, Edinburgh
Printed and bound in Great Britain by
Clays Ltd, Elcograf S.p.A.

Papers used by Robinson are from well-
managed forests and other responsible
sources.

MIX
Paper from
responsible sources
FSC® C104740

Robinson
An imprint of
Little, Brown Book Group
Carmelite House
50 Victoria Embankment
London EC4Y 0DZ

An Hachette UK Company
www.hachette.co.uk

www.littlebrown.co.uk

CONTENTS

ACKNOWLEDGEMENTS

As with any achievement in life, this book is the result of many things, not all of them immediately obvious. It's said that the best way to learn is to teach, and since setting up Alan Hester Associates sixteen years ago I have had the privilege of working with a great many people from all walks of life. They have shared their challenges, their ideas and their experiences with me and fellow learners and their response to my training and coaching has in turn taught me a lot. Some of their stories appear in this book, with names and other details changed to protect their privacy.

Get Out Of Your Own Way is as much my story as theirs, and I would like to acknowledge my family and friends, who have always been there for me. My wife Eunice believed in the concept of this book from the outset and has put up with me locking myself in the office for days on end with my music playing loudly while I wrote, and with much more besides. Thanks to my son Michael, whose knowledge of evolution and much else has opened my eyes to some different ways of viewing this crazy and wonderful world, and to my daughter, Charlotte, for being you, and for having such a positive and generous approach to life. Thanks also to Kim Pottinger for being such a great friend since childhood and many hours of conversation in the curry houses of Reading and beyond.

I would like to personally thank some specific people who helped to make *Get Out Of Your Own Way* a reality. Jackie Jarvis is an excellent business mentor and author, and it's no exaggeration to say that neither this book nor my first one could have happened without her. She identified that writing is my passion, and that I have a story I want to tell, then helped me to get out of my own way for long enough to write them. Alison Harrison and Graham Berry have also been invaluable as part of our monthly business owners' mastermind group. The book also builds on the work of some brilliant authors, whose books I have acknowledged in the bibliography.

Special thanks to Shirley for being an excellent friendly critic, reading each chapter and giving me such valuable feedback, and to Kathy for being positive and supportive the whole way through. I'm lucky to have such great sisters.

Thanks also to Giles Lewis and Nikki Read of How To Books, who put their faith in me in accepting *Management Starts With You* and who have been a knowledgeable and reassuring presence as I worked on my second book for Little, Brown. Jane Donovan, who has copy-edited both of my books, has also been a friendly and helpful presence, and her feedback has made an important contribution to the final product. Amanda Keats has edited both this book and my previous one with clarity and a light touch, while always being on hand with practical responses to all situations. Little, Brown are a lovely company to work with, and everyone I've dealt with there has been friendly, professional and supportive.

INTRODUCTION – GETTING IN YOUR OWN WAY

Do you recognise some of the following statements?

- Everyone else is sorted but I'm not
- Stuff like this always happens to me
- I haven't got the time
- If only *that* could happen then I could do *this*
- That kind of happiness/success/status isn't for the likes of me.

The biggest barrier to success and personal fulfilment is the person looking back at you in the mirror as you get ready for the day ahead. He or she is also the single most powerful person in your life. You may be used to looking elsewhere for the things you want and need, hoping for someone else to do something for you or blaming them when they don't, but in reality there is only one person who can actually make those things happen. The sad thing is, if you're like so many of your fellow human beings you will regularly and repeatedly stop yourself from doing what you most want to do: you will get in your own way.

·····································

The biggest barrier to success and personal fulfilment is the person looking back at you in the mirror as you get ready for the day ahead.

·····································

The world is full of people who have achieved things that we think we ourselves could also achieve but somehow we don't. We may be in the habit of comparing ourselves with those people and feeling inferior or resentful, or we may look for unfair advantages that they have and we don't. We may bemoan fate or luck, or, if we have one, God. We may be plagued by any number of common conditions, such as starting something and not finishing it, making bad decisions or (even worse) no decision at all. We may lack confidence and the root of confidence, which is self-belief. We may not think we deserve success, that there is no point in trying, that we may be ridiculed or judged. These are just a few of the ways in which we get in our own way.

This book is not guaranteed to make you a 'success' – whatever that is – or even to make you 'happy' – however you might define happiness: as I say, only you can do these things. What it *will* do is show you some of the ways in which you might be getting in your own way and actively preventing yourself from doing what you already know is right. We can then work on these to find out:

1 Why we cause the very things we want to avoid
2 Why we do things that are actively 'wrong' for us
3 Why we stop ourselves from doing what we know is 'right'
4 Why it is natural for people to lack self-confidence
5 The fears that cause these bad habits.

There are, inevitably, certain events in our lives that we cannot control, but we can control our response to those events, and we can decide the outcome. I hope this book will be a useful guide for you as you learn how to get out of your own way and become your own best adviser, motivator and friend.

CHAPTER ONE

Stick Or Twist? Change, Risk and Making Decisions

....

Most people don't achieve their goals or ambitions. The author Colin Turner, in his book, Born To Succeed, *makes the awful statement that 'most people go to their graves with their music still inside them.' How sad is that? More importantly, why is that?*

Self-help and positive thinking gurus are fond of saying that our life as it is now is the direct result of all the decisions we have made up to that point. In other words, we are to blame if we find ourselves in a different place than we would like to be.

....

The gurus are right, of course – we always are! – but how does that knowledge make you feel? To be told that it's your own fault because you made the wrong decision last time doesn't really help you to make a better decision next time, does it? It makes you feel embarrassed and inadequate and undermines your confidence even more, so you end up feeling worse about yourself because you've been so stupid in the past. So you can now add a generous helping of guilt to your existing sense of disappointment and unfairness. Now you know how important it is to make the right decision, and how badly you failed before, you need to pick yourself up and do it all again – and of course you have to get it right next time.

Making a decision involves looking at the available evidence, making an assessment of the best outcome possible, making a choice and then committing to the best of the available options. Simple, isn't it? No, it isn't! Decision-making is at the heart of our quest for self-fulfilment, growth and achievement. If you can't or won't make a decision then you are ruling out the possibility of change and improvement, and perhaps denying yourself the opportunities that are all around you. Yet it is probably the main reason why, as Turner says, we don't achieve our potential.

. . . .

The root of all our fears is the fear of failure.

. . . .

A decision is a commitment to do or not to do something specific. It is that element of committing to something that scares us. It seems irrevocable, so once we have made a commitment we feel that we can't unmake it, that it will have inevitable consequences and that we will be powerless to do anything about it. Once that decision is made, we are responsible for what happens next and that responsibility can make us delay or panic; make a knee-jerk decision that we instantly regret or tie ourselves up in knots by second-guessing all the possible consequences. And those consequences weigh so heavily on us that we dread the responsibility of deciding anything of importance.

If our lives really are the result of the decisions we make (and, on the whole, they are) then we had better get pretty damn good at making them, and we had better start right now. Oh heck, that sounded like a decision! Let's work out how we can approach this and start preparing ourselves to be rid of this madness. Let's explore how we can get out of our own way when we have a decision to make, so that we can make decisions that are the right ones for us, and enjoy making them. If that's all right with you, I wouldn't want to offend anyone, or worry them . . .

Why is decision-making so scary?

There are as many reasons for not making a decision as there are people not making them. This chapter, and this book, will hold these reasons up to the light and examine them, and suggest some ways in which we can identify these barriers and either manage them or, better still, remove them completely.

Those same reasons also make us question any decision we do manage to make, making it next to impossible to follow that decision through.

- Do you find that you make a decision and then unmake it straight away?
- Do you find yourself questioning your motives, or your ability, or even your right to make a decision at all?
- Do you find yourself turning things over and over in your head so that what at first seemed obvious now seems complicated, and what was once clear is now so muddled that you don't know what you really think any more?

If you are nodding in agreement with that last point, you have identified one of the most infuriating, unnecessary and destructive ways in which we get in our own way: by undermining ourselves to the extent that we provide our own government, our own opposition and our own press all at the same time. We end up by proposing something, rejecting it and providing our own running commentary so that we argue ourselves to a standstill and make it impossible to move forward with any degree of clarity or confidence.

As in the world of news and other media, the commentary is overwhelmingly critical, and we are more interested in bad news than good, so our internal voice is always negative, prodding and poking away at our self-esteem and confidence. Later in this book we will find out why; at the moment, however, we just need to recognise what that voice is doing and find out how to stop it from coming between us and our happiness.

What if I make a wrong decision?

This is the root of all our fears: the fear of failure or getting it wrong. The very phrase 'wrong decision' is loaded with regret, guilt, remorse and all kinds of negative feelings. If you enter a decision-making process with those emotions in your head, you are virtually guaranteeing that you will make a wrong decision – or, at least, that you will make the decision for all the wrong reasons, which is often the same thing.

·······························

Don't be afraid of making a 'wrong' decision. We only grow through facing challenges and overcoming them, even if we've caused those challenges ourselves by making a mistake.

·······························

Of course, in retrospect, some decisions we make won't bring about the outcome we wanted. For example, we might apply for a job thinking it's the perfect one for us, then realise on the first morning that it will never work out (guilty as charged on that one!). So, is it a disaster? In my case, I suffered some stressful and difficult times and was glad when it all came to a not particularly pleasant end, but it was far from all bad news. What I learnt from that experience was priceless in helping me to make my next career move. I would go so far as to say that I would never have been able to set up my own business if it hadn't been for the harsh lessons and the delivery and problem-solving skills I was forced to develop while in that role. These were skills I would never have gained had I stayed in the secure job I had left to take that one.

Had I stayed where I was, I would have been comfortable, safe and would perhaps have grown a little 'flabby' and complacent. So, was my move a 'wrong decision' or was it part of my journey? We only grow through facing challenges and overcoming them, even if we've caused those challenges ourselves by making a mistake. The often misquoted Darwinian principle of survival of the fittest applies here: it's not necessarily the fittest who survive, it's those who are able to adapt to the challenging environment they find themselves in. Often, even our mistakes are good.

....

If you do anything at all, you will make mistakes. If you are doing something that you are unfamiliar with, you will get it wrong a few times before you get it right and while failure is overrated, it's one of our very best learning tools.

....

Forgive your mistakes

....

'The greatest mistake you can make in life is to be continually fearing you will make one.' Elbert Hubbard

....

If you do anything at all, you will make mistakes. If you are doing something that you are unfamiliar with, you will get it wrong a few times before you get it right and while failure is overrated, it's also one of our very best learning tools.

We all make mistakes. We may even make some every day. Does that make us bad people? Don't conflate these two unrelated things: if you make a mistake it doesn't make you a bad person, it just makes you a human being. If you have done the very best you can and things still haven't worked out, there is no shame in that. If you go in for excessive self-immolation then you are on the way to one of the most ridiculous ways of getting in your own way; this is to heap blame on yourself to the point where you think you're the worst person in the world and can't be trusted to do anything right.

. . . .

Don't conflate these two unrelated things: if you make a mistake it doesn't make you a bad person, it just makes you a human being.

. . . .

You did your best, it didn't work out. Instead of worrying yourself into ever smaller circles, use your head. Think about what happened and why; take the learning out of it and go again.

Why no decision is still a decision

Our lack of decisiveness is a form of self-protection: if we don't make a decision then we can't be blamed when it goes wrong. Unfortunately for us, this doesn't work. Most things in life – I would argue, *everything* in life – comes with a built-in time limit. Opportunities come with their own lifespan and if we miss the window of opportunity, it closes.

If we put off making a decision until we are absolutely certain it's the right one, we will never make that decision because we can never guarantee that it will turn out to be the right one. If we make no decision, we are actually making a decision: we are deciding to allow the opportunity to pass, for control of our life to be handed over to fate, or chance, or even to someone else. We are deciding to put the existing routine on repeat instead of allowing a new tune to play and a new future to emerge.

Think about the things in your life that you most regret and they will be the things you didn't do, the commitments you never made, the chances you didn't take. Don't be a bystander in your own life.

Getting in the way of change

Change is an important word in our quest to get out of our own way. Whenever I ask a group to react to the prospect of a change happening in their lives, whether at home or in the workplace, their instant response is always the same. Typical comments include: Why? Not again? I hate it. What's the point? Leave me alone! It takes a number of these negative comments before someone ventures that change might not be a bad thing, that it could be interesting, or perhaps a good thing, or even that it's about time something changed. People virtually never respond to imminent change by thinking: 'Things are about to change – great!'

Even people whose lives are anything but happy or fulfilling, who are crying out for change and are working with me because they want to make changes in their lives will react in the same way. So, unhappy people resist change, even though they need things to change to enable them to be happier. This is important: fear of change actively prevents us from doing things that can make our lives better.

When we fear change, what are we really afraid of? We fear exposure to danger. We may not see it that way, but every time we place ourselves in a new situation that asks something of us that may not have been asked before, we expose ourselves to risk. It may be that we are worried that we won't be able to cope; that we don't have the ability or resources to deal with the new situation, or that we might fail or even look stupid. It is this element of danger that harks back to earlier times in human evolution when risk of failure could mean being killed or even eaten, and we have taken this ancient instinct for survival with us into situations where the dangers are very different and, mostly, not remotely as serious as we imagine.

In her influential book *Feel the Fear and Do It Anyway*, Susan Jeffers argues that we build up in our minds an expectation of danger or of bad consequences on the basis of little or no evidence; that we predict negative outcomes and can attach them to something quite innocuous. Therefore, as we attempt something difficult or something we tried to do once before and 'failed', we decide beforehand that we can't handle it.

This is a natural human response but it doesn't necessarily make it a useful one. At its most serious, we can build these responses up

GET OUT OF YOUR OWN WAY

into phobias that effectively paralyse us and prevent us from doing the most ordinary things. I have worked with people on my self-esteem and confidence programmes who couldn't drive because they had once been involved in an accident, couldn't attend a job interview panel because they had a nasty experience with their previous bosses, couldn't get onto a bus or shop in a supermarket without having panic attacks. They then avoided any situations that risked exposure to the things they had become obsessed about.

At the more common and less serious end of the spectrum we can easily become fearful of any situation that we perceive as carrying the risk of failure or embarrassment, or that may make us uncomfortable in some other way. Jeffers argues that if we acknowledge those feelings but do it anyway, we can look back on our 'failure' in the knowledge that we not only survived it but learnt from it, achieving something on the way and reducing its power to frighten us into submission. When you look back on something that made you nervous, it is never as big or scary as it was before you made the attempt. If, on the other hand, you avoid it, next time you face your fears they have grown and the next attempt is not only scarier but the likelihood of us making the attempt has receded further into the distance.

Change is continuous and inevitable so to pretend otherwise means that you will be likely to resist, avoid or deny the possibility of change. All these behaviours are counterproductive. If we fail to engage with the changes in our lives we are literally saying that we want to be a passenger – we are abdicating responsibility for our own life. It's the difference between being a passenger in a car, wishing that the driver would take more care and not drive so fast, or being in the driver's seat ourselves, controlling where we are going and what decisions we are taking as we drive.

If any of us were to think about our lives today compared to our lives five years ago we would be able to point to any number of things that are different. Change is happening all around us and it is happening to us too. As we will see later in this chapter, if we do nothing ourselves to directly bring about change, it will still happen. People come and go in our lives, our surroundings change around us and our friends and families are doing different things. At work it is unusual for any organisation to go even a couple of years without some fairly major change, at least some of which is going to directly or indirectly affect you. So, however much we may want to stick our heads in the sand, change still happens.

Outside of home or work, change and upheaval seem to be happening faster than ever. I remember an old cartoon in which a mean father refuses his son's request for a new atlas (remember those?), arguing that he can't buy him one 'until world affairs are more settled'. Looking at the world today, that new atlas would be further away than ever.

Whether or not we welcome these changes in our lives we still have to deal with them. When I work with people who find that they automatically recoil from the idea of imminent change, we then spend some time understanding why. This is a common theme for this book: before we can begin to get out of our own way and stop putting up barriers, we need to understand how we put up those barriers and, even more importantly, why. Unless we understand the causes of our frustration with ourselves and our lives, we will find it impossible to break through and come out the other side.

....

If you make no decision at all, you are still making a decision. Everything in life comes with a built-in time limit. Opportunities come with their own lifespan and if we miss the window of opportunity, it closes.

....

Here are three of the most important aspects of change that we need to get to grips with. They hold the key to our ability to properly engage with change, welcome it and make good decisions so that change works for us and not against us:

Control is a key factor in our attitude towards change. The instant barriers we put up are a result of us feeling that the situation is out of our control. If we feel that something is being done *to* us, rather than *with* us, we fear it and reject it. We feel insecure. We resent the people we hold responsible for pushing us into something we're not comfortable with.

If we view change in this way then we are voluntarily putting ourselves in the role of victim because we are waiting for others to decide our fate. We are behaving like the passenger in the car, worrying about what might happen and being dependent on someone else. It's possible to live your whole life like this; waiting, watching and worrying, and not taking responsibility for your own journey.

The moment we decide (and it *is* a decision) to take a different view, we will get a different result. As Shakespeare once said: 'Nothing is good or ill but thinking makes it so,' and he was a pretty good judge of character. Perception is reality, so if you perceive change as bad, it will be. If you perceive it as good, or simply as potentially interesting, you can indulge another human characteristic – curiosity. A great question to ask ourselves is: 'What would happen if. . .?' What if I got involved? What if I found out more about it? What if I could influence the way things go? What could be in this for me? When presented with a change, you are making a decision as to how you want to react to it.

If we want something to happen, we need to take some steps to make it happen. We can be in an unhappy situation and feel sorry for ourselves, blaming the world, or the government, or the people in our lives for not doing anything to help us. Or we can decide what we want to do, what we will or will not accept, and do something about it. We've all had these flashpoints at some point in our lives, where we decide enough is enough and take some action. As we will see in later chapters, taking action can mean that we start doing something positive or stop doing something negative. Either way we instantly feel better when we put ourselves in the driving seat.

• •

The moment we take control of a situation is the moment we stop worrying and start doing.

• •

By the way, we don't even need to be in a position of authority to make a difference; just deciding to exercise control over ourselves is enough. Then we can manage the situation, and the moment we take control of a situation is the moment we stop worrying and start doing.

Understanding something is the first step towards dealing with it. We fear what we can't understand, and if we fear something, our instinct is to avoid it. We can't make a sensible decision on something we haven't taken the trouble to understand because we don't have the information we need. We are relying on gut instinct and not on facts, or even interpretation of facts. There is nothing wrong with gut instinct – it's a powerful thing and a great asset to anyone who needs to make an instant decision. However, if you can add knowledge and experience to gut instinct then you get incredible results.

If you are in a confusing situation, or you have a choice between two options, taking the time to learn and understand helps in many ways. Knowledge is power, knowledge increases understanding, knowledge removes fear and without knowledge, you are guessing.

Involvement is better than disengagement. If you get involved in something, you have the chance to influence it. Involvement means action, and without action nothing can happen – apart from what happens to you as a result of actions that have been taken by someone else.

Comfort zones – staying where you are because you're used to it

Each of us has his or her personal comfort zone. This is the place in our lives, physically, intellectually or emotionally, that we always come back to when faced with a choice or a challenge. We naturally retreat to our comfort zone for some very sensible reasons: we feel safe there because we already know how to live in it, we know what to expect and are confident that we can deal with it. However, if we stay in our comfort zone in order to protect ourselves from risk and failure then we will never take a risk or challenge ourselves to master a new skill or situation.

The comfort zone is not always comfortable. Sometimes it is simply that we are used to it and know we can handle it. This is why people stay in boring jobs way beyond the time that they should have moved on to something else, and why they stay in significantly more damaging situations. I don't believe most of us stay where we are because we expect things to improve, but simply because we prefer to continue with something that is bearable than take the risk of finding something even worse. We know how to wake up in the morning and face a day of boredom (or worse) because we've done it so often already; we don't know what it's like to do something we've never tried before and that we might not instantly be good at or comfortable with. In this way we put up with something that doesn't excite or enthuse us in order to avoid the risk of failure.

A lot has been said and written in the past few decades about children being over-protected by concerned parents to the extent that they fail to develop the coping skills they would otherwise learn from being made to feel uncomfortable from time to time. Parents want to protect their children, and we want to protect ourselves, all of which is understandable, but if we remove all risk, we don't get the opportunity to test ourselves and grow. There needs to be a balance between children being feral and put at unacceptable risk on the one hand or being cossetted on the other. As adults, we also need to find a productive balance between risk and reward.

· ·

Take only calculated risks

In my twenties I worked in a Civil Service office. The job was secure, I had some good friends and while the work was a bit routine, I became quite comfortable. One summer, a friend and I decided to spend our holidays on an archaeological dig (he was a medieval history graduate and I had enjoyed digs before). Towards the end of the dig, he said to me: 'I want to keep doing this. When I get back, I'm going to resign and go on another one.' He was true to his word and resigned on our first day back. When a colleague asked how on earth he could take the risk of giving up a safe job for such an uncertain future his reply was simple and logical.

'Last week I was a civil servant. Now I'm an archaeologist with a four-week contract. Then I'll think about what to do next.'

Of course, behind this devastatingly simple logic there was a particular set of circumstances, and it's only fair to you if I'm open about these. He lived at home with his parents. He cycled everywhere. He remains to this day the only person I know who ever had a letter from his bank manager (yes, they used to write letters then), telling him that he had too much money in his current account! So he had no responsibilities and wasn't risking his family's future. He could afford to be 'irresponsible'.

In case you're wondering what happened to him, he did a few temporary jobs on archaeological digs, and during one of them met someone who ran a war game company in Nottingham and invited him to work there. While there he met a girl he fell in love with. So his decision to leave a secure job, which most people thought was rash and foolish, had many benefits for him: it freed him from a boring job, gave him new experiences, made him new friends, got him a girl, a new place to live, more money and a specialist job in a young and growing industry doing something he loved.

. . . .

I'm not suggesting that we should risk everything in a series of leaps of faith, or that we should risk our family's security through being reckless. The advice that we should never gamble more than we can afford to lose is good advice. That said, we can easily find ourselves hiding behind risks that aren't really risks at all, or are so small compared to the potential benefits that taking a bit of a chance is a no-brainer.

If you have an ambition that you want to achieve, or even simply an experience that you crave but have never had the time or the opportunity to enjoy, ask yourself what is stopping you from doing it. Once you've identified your barrier, ask yourself if it is a real one, or something you've built up in your own head. Susan Jeffers has a phrase for fear which she turns into an acronym: FEAR stands for False Evidence Appearing Real. We anticipate the worst, exaggerate potential problems and expect them to happen; then, because our brains are programmed to seek pleasure and avoid pain, we anticipate that our attempt would end badly so we withdraw. We are beaten before we have even started.

What do we really want to be or do?

This is probably the single biggest reason for underachievement: the failure to set a proper goal. If you don't know what you want, how can you work towards it? There are many reasons for not setting a clear goal – including not allowing yourself to do so because you've already convinced yourself you won't achieve it!

At this point I want to be clear about something: there is no requirement on anyone to be ambitious or competitive. This is not a book about how to finish top and beat the other guy, it is about how to achieve what you want to achieve – for yourself, for your family, maybe for your employer. Your ambition could be to be the best parent you could possibly be, or the best guitar player, or to run a personal best (PB) in your next half-marathon, or to charge what you're worth. The important thing is that there is something you want to achieve that will make you feel more fulfilled once you've achieved it, and that you don't deny yourself the higher self-esteem and confidence on offer by allowing yourself to get in your own way.

People sometimes argue that we shouldn't set ambitious goals as we are doomed to disappointment when we fail. It's a fair point. I know I will never play for England in an Ashes Test (I was never good enough and now I'm too old), but if I had genuinely had that ambition as a boy, I could have given it a real go and if I had, I bet I could have got much closer to it than I ever did. My biggest real ambition was to be an author; thankfully, you can do that much later in life, and this is my second book.

I once gave a talk at a school and a boy at the back (they're *always* at the back) wanted to prove that you couldn't achieve anything through positive thinking and hard work. He said he wanted to be an astronaut and folded his arms, pleased to have said something ridiculous and unachievable. When I asked if he was prepared to study maths, physics and chemistry at A-level and work towards top grades his expression changed a little. Was he prepared to work out at the gym and eat a healthy diet too? The smile disappeared. Would he be prepared to move to America and apply to join their space programme? Like a lot of people he wanted to prove that nothing could be achieved so there was no point in trying. After all, if we don't try, we can't fail. Also, if we can prove that there's no point in trying then we don't have to try at all. He was trying to prove that he was clever and right, and to do so without the inconvenience of having to take responsibility for actually doing anything at all. There's a little of that boy's thinking in all of us.

So, why do we find it so difficult to set a clear goal and work towards it? There are many reasons. This chapter has already identified a few of them and others will appear throughout this book. I believe that the most common reasons for not deciding on a goal and committing to it are also some of the clearest examples of how we continually get in our own way.

Lack of confidence in my own ability. I'm bound to fail, so why not save myself the embarrassment and not even try in the first place?

Lack of self-esteem. What right have I got to ask for that? I'm not worthy of this kind of success, it's not for the likes of me. I mustn't get above my station, who do I think I am?

Lack of commitment. It seems like a lot of effort, is it worth it? What's the point? Who am I kidding anyway?

I might succeed. What if I do, by some fluke, manage to achieve it? What if it isn't all that I dreamed it would be? What if it doesn't make me happy?

....

'I knew all along that the prize I had set my life on was not worth the winning.' Major Dobbin in Vanity Fair *by William Makepeace Thackeray*

....

The above are all forms of self-sabotage. Self-fulfilling prophecies, they drain away the passion, courage and commitment you need in order to become what you are capable of being. It is because of these that so many of us deny ourselves the joy of doing what we were born to do. And for those of you who don't think we were born for any specific purpose at all, would you prefer to chug along aimlessly, frustrated and tired, or find that sense of purpose that makes you truly you?

Decide what you want to do and then start doing it. Identify the things you need to do and start doing them. Find out how you need to behave and start behaving like it. Work out what you need to have and take steps to get it. This could be making time, learning new skills, doing some research, working on your attitudes and beliefs or simply having a go at something and

21

learning from your successes and failures. Start doing the things that will help you to get there and stop doing the things that won't. Forget about the self-doubts and the problems you might encounter along the way.

CHAPTER TWO

Your Brain: A User's Guide

Your brain is a complex and powerful thing. It is capable of more than you could possibly imagine. Even with all the recent advances in computing it is quicker, more capable and more multi-talented than the most advanced computer yet produced. The brain's capacity for storing and processing information is, as far as we know, limitless. All that power and potential is available to you right now.

So, how come you don't feel enormously successful? How come you don't have ridiculously high self-esteem and confidence? How come you don't wake up every morning, eat all the right things, exercise your mind and body for peak condition and set and achieve half a dozen goals that bring you health, wealth and eternal happiness? Why is life often a bit of a struggle, work tedious and unfulfilling but nevertheless so demanding that you have no energy left to pursue your dreams when you head home at the end of the day? Why, with all that processing power at your disposal, do you worry that you've frittered away so much time without getting any closer to where you want to be?

We need to acknowledge these issues and face up to them if we are to make friends with our brain and tap into this enormously powerful resource. So, let's start by understanding how your brain works and whether or not you are really in control of your thoughts and actions.

· ·

Your brain is a hugely powerful super-computer, but it depends entirely on the programming you put into it.

· ·

At this point I will put my cards on the table. In this chapter, I will try to separate the myths about the human brain from the facts, but to be honest I'm less interested in the science (fascinating though it is) than the practicalities. I will be focusing on what we need to know about the brain in order to help us understand what we can do to harness its potential and avoid its problems. We need to know how we can maintain our brain so that it performs well for us and gets us to where we want to be. Older readers will remember those books that helped us to change the oil and repair our cars; those volumes didn't explain how a carburettor worked, but told us enough to know how to fix it if it went wrong. This chapter is, in effect, a *Haynes Owners' Manual for the Brain*.

We only use a small portion of our potential

It is often said that we only use around 5 per cent of our brain, with 95 per cent remaining untouched. It may feel like that at times, but scientifically this is not true and we are in fact using most of our brains most of the time. However, there is a kernel of truth in this myth as we only use a fraction of the potential of our brain to work for us and help us to achieve.

One of the reasons we fail to tap into this huge potential is that human beings are quick to form habits. We find a way of looking at the world, and a way of dealing with it, that works – or at least appears to – so there is no pressure on us to do anything differently. A little later in this chapter we will look at where these habits come from and how they form, but it is clear that if, as the now famous saying goes, we always do what we've always done, we will always get the same results.

Why does your brain work against you?

Your brain can do almost anything, so why does it often choose the very things that damage you and cause you problems? It's your very own super-computer yet it seems to spend much of its time undermining you and preventing you from doing what's best for you. In fact, you have probably spent an awful lot of time doing all the wrong things and not doing all the right things – I know I have. In writing these words I feel like the Monty Python psychiatrist attempting to reassure others that their errant behaviour is normal: 'Who can honestly say,' he declared in his pompous, self-satisfied voice, 'that at one time or another he hasn't set fire to some great public building? I know I have. Get it out in the open. I know I have.'

....

Because we make up our minds about people and beliefs in advance, we often defend ourselves against threats that may not actually exist.

....

We form beliefs and turn those beliefs into tablets of stone. Later in this chapter we will see that the subconscious mind has a powerful role in dictating how we respond in any situation, and that power is based solidly on the information we give to our brain. If we believe that a particular type of person is bad or dangerous, we will expect bad or dangerous behaviour from them and will inwardly reject anything they say. If we have had a bad experience of a particular situation and are facing a situation that feels similar, we will anticipate the return of those same bad feelings. We therefore gear up to defend ourselves against threats that may not actually exist.

We have a dialogue going on in our head all the time. We will see in Chapter Five how cognitive dissonance works and how we screen out inconvenient facts and opinions that get in the way of our world view. For now, I want to concentrate on the way our brain interprets the instructions we give it and what that does to our ability to react to external stimuli.

If we have already drawn our conclusions then we don't need to think any more, we've already made up our mind. Therefore, anything that happens or anything said to us is processed through the prism of our existing beliefs and we draw the pre-programmed conclusion, whether or not it is appropriate to the specific information we are receiving. Our brain is simply carrying out the instructions we have already installed in it. After all, when a computer system goes wrong, people often say, 'Rubbish in, rubbish out,' don't they?

In this way, we can hear a person talking to us but interpret their words very differently from the way they were intended. Often we can take offence where none was intended, and we can reject something simply because of our predetermined judgement on the source of the information. We have prejudged the situation, and this is the route of prejudice. So in any given situation we are inclined to prejudge rather than sift and analyse. It has been proved beyond reasonable doubt that human beings do not on the whole make logical decisions, we make emotional ones and dress them up as logic. We see what we want to see and hear what we want to hear because we take on board only what we have instructed our brain to take on board.

Where do our beliefs, expectations and values come from?

I have said that we are responsible for the instructions that we put into our brain, but in fact we are the sum total of all the experiences, beliefs and values we have absorbed in our lives up to this point. It is safe to assume that for much of our childhood and formative years we simply 'take in' these messages and internalise them as the way things are. We learn from the significant others in our lives and from the totality of our experiences. So, let's look at some of these people and the impact they have on us.

Parents are the most obvious source of the raw material our brains are given to work with. Along with, of course, the genetic inheritance we also receive from them and through them other relatives. The actor Warren Mitchell, who played Alf Garnett in the seventies sitcom *Till Death Do Us Part*, was a very different man from the racist bigot he portrayed on screen. Mitchell, rather than Garnett, argued in an appearance on the *Parkinson* talk show that to raise children in strict systems of belief in which they were encouraged to think anyone outside of that belief system was at best an enemy and at worst not fully human, was a form of child abuse. His reasoning was that such children had no alternative in what they believed and were set on a path in which they had no choice but to believe what they were told and to act on that basis. This, he argued, was behind much of the religious and nationalist bigotry and violence in the world. It was, he felt, the manipulation or brainwashing of a captive audience.

Of course, as parents, our motivation is to do the very best for our children, and instilling what we perceive to be the right values and behaviours is integral to us doing our job of preparing them to function successfully and happily in our society. But Mitchell's wider point is a good one: it is very difficult to escape from the programming installed in our computer/brain at such a young age and reinforced for most of our formative years. Benign as our parents' advice and guidance may be, and valuable as so much of it is, it was placed in our brains by someone other than ourselves. Therefore some of our values and beliefs are 'passed down' to us as fact, when they may be nothing of the kind.

From the child's point of view, we want to please our parents, as they are the source of our security. Therefore we adopt behaviours most likely to please them. Again, in most cases this is a natural and positive arrangement, but elements may prove problematic for us in later life.

The Personal Drivers model from Transactional Analysis (TA) is interesting in this respect. Each of the five drivers of behaviour is about our relations with others: we are driven by the need to Be Perfect, Be Strong, Please People, Hurry Up or Try Hard. If we feel that we are failing to live up to our particular standard for ourselves, we can become stressed and unhappy. However, these drivers are all about how we think we need to behave in relation to others, they are not about what we want and what is important to us, so our lives are spent trying to fit into a straitjacket designed for the benefit of others and not for us.

I worked with a woman who came to my course as a referral from a mental health charity. She had always wanted to be an artist and had won a place at art college, where she was scheduled to hold an exhibition of her paintings. This was the highlight of her life, and was what she had wanted to do from an early age. What did she do instead? She left art college early and cancelled her exhibition before spending some months drifting in and out of temporary jobs that held no interest for her and into spells of unemployment. When I met her months had turned into years and in her late twenties she had no confidence and no sense of direction: being an artist had become a pipe dream.

She described a childhood with a lazy and self-indulgent father who took no notice of her, declining to come to school for parents' evenings and not even attending displays of her paintings or watching her in school plays. The only time he ever paid attention to her or told her she was a good girl was when she brought him cups of tea, went to the shop to buy him a newspaper or made him breakfast in bed. She had no sense of self-worth at all, only feeling worthwhile when she did something for someone else.

Her brain had interpreted this as an instruction in what to expect from life and she learnt to behave in accordance with that expectation. Seen in this light it's no mystery that her brain chose the very moment when she was about to fulfil her dreams to sabotage her as spectacularly and decisively as it could.

We are all labelled as children. Most of the time it is harmless, and often positive, but think about the impact of some of these 'labels' on the child as he or she grows into an adult and becomes a parent, an employee, a partner or friend: the strong one, the quiet one, the naughty one, 'trouble', 'good', greedy, kind, loud, fun or serious. This woman had never made the connection between the instruction to please people, reinforced throughout her childhood, and the low value she placed on her own needs and wants. Making that connection was an important step in allowing her to start making decisions for herself, the first of which was to re-enter paid work and start to become independent.

Peer group. Once we begin to spend more of our time outside the home and connect with a peer group of others of our own age we are exposed to different influences. This is where we learn some new social norms and values. In the long-running animated comedy *The Simpsons*, when Bart Simpson gets in with a bad crowd who pressure him into some potentially serious wrongdoing he goes to his father Homer for advice. Homer helpfully tells him 'nothing is more important than being popular'. Peer pressure brings us another set of norms and behaviours that we absorb into our super-computer, only to become a further set of instructions for what to think, do and feel in later life.

Media. In the age of smartphones and tablets, media is a bigger influence on us than ever before. Images and messages enter our conscious and subconscious minds insistently and constantly, and play their part in how we see the world. We all know that news media, whether on TV, in newspapers or on other platforms is predominantly focused on bad news rather than good. This can contribute to the feeling shared by many of us that the world is unsafe and we should always expect the worst.

The average evening's TV viewing shows us three or four murders, either real or fictional, and plenty of other unsettling images. I'm not arguing that this is a bad thing, I'm just saying this is so, and that these images enter our brains as part of the fabric of the society in which we grow up and operate. Look no further than the Ice Bucket Challenge in the summer of 2014 for evidence of the power of the media (for good or ill) to directly influence behaviour. For several weeks, Facebook was full of videos of people pouring water over each other before the 'victim' then named several friends or connections who would be next. Very few people resisted the challenge: we need to fit in and belong, it's what makes us human.

Why is self-talk negative?

In Chapter Three, we will look in detail at self-talk and the instructions we give to our brains. We see that our instinctive or knee-jerk responses are usually negative: we are overly critical of ourselves, we exaggerate danger or we assume we will fail. If our world view is that life is dangerous and unfair, or that we need to be cautious at all times and have a safety-first approach towards everything, it is logical that our self-talk will reflect that. I remember my dad advising me to work in the Post Office, because he saw it as a secure place to work. To him security and predictability was everything.

Our parents are concerned for our safety, and will unwittingly give safety-first messages to their children that are bound to influence their approach to life. That's good; if we're a parent we want our children to behave safely and sensibly. We also want them to take calculated risks and enjoy themselves.

When we have our first child we are by definition inexperienced in the art of parenting and so we learn from others (our own parents) and the rest of it we make up as we go along. When our first child heads off at full pelt for the climbing frame at the local park we say 'be careful' – a message that the child is likely to take on board (eventually). By the time our second child is going out to play we have less time and have relaxed a little, so we are more likely to tell him or her to 'have fun'. This is why the eldest child is often more serious and careful than those who come after. We all take these messages on board, our computer processes them and we learn to behave accordingly.

How do we change unhelpful attitudes, beliefs and expectations?

Are we in control of our brains, or do our brains control us? There's enough debate here to fill several books, but in line with my stated intentions for this book I want to stay focused on what we can control.

All the input I've been describing from parents, peers and media influences has taken a lifetime of reinforcement to become firmly entrenched in our brain. They are so well-rooted that they have become the prism through which we view everything. In effect we already know the answer to every question, and that answer can be found by searching the database of information that we already possess. Put simply, we rule out answers that don't fit with our preconceived ideas.

Is that a problem for us? We'll see later when we look in more detail at the impact of our self-talk on our ability to respond positively to opportunities and difficulties. If our brain's response, however, is to tell us that we don't deserve to succeed, or we shouldn't be trying, or that our needs are not as important as the needs of others, then perhaps it is a problem.

....

Our subconscious mind makes virtually all our decisions for us. We've already given it all the information it needs and all it does is tell the conscious mind what to do. If we can programme the subconscious for success or achievement, or open-mindedness or learning then it will ask the conscious mind to go and deliver it.

....

If our belief is that the world is a sad and dangerous place, there is plenty of evidence for that without even opening our front door, through the news and other sources, and from the losses we all suffer in our lives. If we feel that failure is inevitable, and that failing in a particular part of our life makes us a failure in every part of it, then it is a problem as it will prevent us from making the attempt. Luckily, it doesn't need to take another lifetime to replace unhelpful beliefs and habits with new ones that will help us to move on and take the calculated risks we need to take.

Our subconscious mind is the key to changing our thought patterns and influencing positive behaviour. The role of our subconscious is to instruct our conscious mind how to think and behave. In effect, the subconscious mind makes virtually all our decisions for us. We've already given it all the information it needs and all it does is tell the conscious mind what to do. If we can programme the subconscious for success or achievement, or open-mindedness or learning then it will ask the conscious mind to go and deliver it.

We can only hold one thought in our head at a time
. . . .
We can only hold one thought in our head at any one time, so we are governed by the nature of the thought that we are holding.
. . . .
Although we can move quickly from one thought to another, we can only hold one thought in our head at any given time. What this means is that we are governed by the nature of the thought that we are holding. What we think becomes what we do, and what we do leads to the results we get. So it is vital for our success that we don't allow that thought to be a negative one, or a lazy one, or even a counterproductive one.

Techniques such as affirmation and visualisation (of which more later) enable us to replace negative thoughts with productive ones. We can literally out-talk our negative thoughts if we focus enough on the positive ones.

· ·

What we think becomes what we do, and what we do leads to the results we get.

· ·

Cognitive Behavioural Therapy (CBT) is extremely helpful in enabling us to control our thoughts instead of being controlled by them. CBT works by inviting us to identify the automatic assumptions that govern our behaviour. Some of the most destructive things our minds do include:

Catastrophising. If something goes wrong, or is less than perfect, we see it as a total disaster. One thing didn't work out, so nothing ever will. The world is a terrible place, you are completely worthless and there's nothing anyone can do about it.

Feeling overwhelmed by trying to tackle everything at once. If we perceive a task to be so vast and complex that we don't know where to begin then we will avoid it. CBT encourages us to break big problems down into small steps and to tackle each aspect independently to avoid this sense of being overwhelmed by the feeling that we have to deal with everything at once.

Establishing destructive patterns. This usually involves assuming a link between two unrelated things and conflating them. For example: 'I've failed, therefore I'm a failure. I'll always be a failure. I'm useless'.

Seeking reassurance. Due to our basic lack of confidence and low self-esteem we continually need to be told that there's nothing to worry about. We seek reassurance and get it, but the instant we've been reassured we start to doubt ourselves again and we need more reassurance.

All of these are common problems for most of us and don't mean we're unwell or in need of treatment. We all feel like that from time to time. It's part of being human – infuriating, brilliant, frustrating, wonderful, conflicted creatures that we are! The above are also very good examples of how our brain plays tricks on us and prevents us from being effective and living full, anxiety-free and happy lives.

Your Brain: A User's Guide:
Takeaways from Chapter Two

★ Your brain is a hugely powerful super-computer, but it depends entirely on the programming you put into it

★ **Because we make up our minds about people and beliefs in advance, we often defend ourselves against threats that may not actually exist**

★ Our subconscious mind makes virtually all our decisions for us. We've already given it all the information it needs and all it does is tell the conscious mind what to do. If we can programme the subconscious for success or achievement, or open-mindedness or learning then it will ask the conscious mind to go and deliver it

★ **We can only hold one thought in our head at any one time, so we are governed by the nature of the thought that we are holding**

★ What we think becomes what we do, and what we do leads to the results we get.

CHAPTER THREE

Self-Talk and the Self-fulfilling Prophecy

'I'm a fat, ugly, hideous monster.' There, that's quite a statement, isn't it? It was delivered by a young woman attending a self-esteem course I ran a few years ago at a mental health charity. She said it in response to me asking people to share their current self-talk and, having said it, she folded her arms and stared at me with what I can only describe as a challenging and, interestingly, *smug* expression.

What do you think she was really saying, and what was behind both the smugness (strange word in this context) and the challenge?

Let's put this into context. This was a four-day course on self-esteem, confidence and success for people recovering from mental health conditions and the comment was made during a session on self-talk and the role it plays in our sense of self-worth. I've run similar sessions for people who find themselves long-term unemployed, for drug users, unemployed executives, women returning to work after a career break and those simply looking to make changes in their lives.

To consider what that young woman said, its intended effect on me and actual impact on her, we need to understand what self-talk is, where it comes from and how it affects our choices in life and the outcomes we get as a result of our own self-talk.

Self-talk is a 'running commentary' on your life

What is self-talk? Self-talk is, quite literally, what you say to yourself. It's the voice in your head that tells you who you are, what you are capable of, and how you see the world and your place in it. These messages tend to be, for reasons already discussed earlier, overwhelmingly negative for the vast majority of people.

We tell ourselves that we can't do something, that we will never be able to do it, that the world is unfair. We decide what other people think of us and what we think of ourselves. We compare ourselves against others and the comparison is unflattering. What self-talk is doing is fundamental to our mission to get out of our own way. Self-talk is a direct instruction we give to ourselves to behave in accordance with a set of beliefs about the world and ourselves; as we then act in accordance with those beliefs we are making certain that those beliefs are proved to be true.

The subconscious mind is lazy. Powerful, yes, but fundamentally lazy. Its job is to carry out the instructions we give it so if the instruction is to reassure you that yes, you are stupid and no, your idea for a new business or arts project is not possible, then let's prove it as quickly and conclusively as possible and move on.

As we will later see in Chapter Five on listening, the best way to avoid learning something new is not to listen to it in the first place. Self-talk is a highly effective way of closing down all options and keeping you on the path you're already on. If you've bought this book because you want to make some changes in your life, then understanding your self-talk and replacing those negative instructions with positive ones is going to be one of your biggest challenges, and one of the best things you can do. Let's return to our 'hideous' friend for a while to help us understand the power of self-talk before looking at ways that we can turn that power into a positive for you.

Absolutes. A common feature of self-talk is our tendency to deal only in absolutes. Self-talk often features words like 'always' and 'never', just in case we might mistakenly get above our station and start thinking we might be able to change something for the better. If something is absolute then there is no point in challenging it, and the more absolute the better. No one likes us; everyone hates us; we have nothing of interest to say; we can't even make a decent cup of tea; we are not clever enough; we don't have the right background; good things don't happen to people like me . . . The young woman on my training course wasn't 'a little bit overweight', she was a 'fat, ugly, hideous monster' – that's about as absolute as you can get.

....

People can help someone who's overweight, but they can't help a monster. That's the power of self-talk.

....

So, what did that thinking achieve for her? What was her subconscious trying to ensure? As we talked, it emerged that the young woman's father had paid for a personal dietician for her, a personal trainer and a personal counsellor. She was also attending regular sessions with the mental health charity for group therapy, social interaction and mutual support. That's an awful lot of help for one person to have. But it made no difference to her weight, her emotional state or her situation. Why?

It became clear to me that she was totally committed to preventing anyone from helping her, and that now included me and the other members of her group. The more people tried to help, the more deeply she resisted. Her outburst came right at the end of the day, having declined earlier to share her self-talk at the time of the session. She waited until near the end of the day when she could be confident that no one would challenge her. Although in the few minutes remaining I was able to get the details of her father's efforts to support her, there wasn't time to talk more deeply about her issues. I told her that we would be covering some topics the next day that would help her. She didn't show.

The young woman was heavily invested in staying exactly where she was. No matter how much her father, her dietician, her trainer, her counsellor, her charity, her fellow group members or I were willing or able to help, she knew it would make no difference. Why? Because she had already decided it wouldn't. People can help someone who's overweight, but they can't help a monster. That's the power of self-talk. Imagine if she could have turned all that willpower, belief and passion in a positive direction.

Self-talk is always right. Let's examine how self-talk works. If I say that no one will be interested in what I have to say, and I'm about to go to a social or networking event, I will behave according to that belief. Someone who has nothing to offer to others is unlikely to walk up to another person and start a conversation. I am much more likely to go and get a drink, stand or sit in the corner of the room, or even go outside if that's an option. At the very least I will make a beeline for someone I already know and talk to them.

Will others approach me? Possibly one or two people whose self-talk tells them that they are good in social situations and enjoy meeting new people. Will they stay very long? I doubt it, as I will be behaving in accordance with my own secret 'script' that says no one is genuinely interested in what I have to say. At the end of the evening, I have proved that I was right about my social abilities and will avoid such events in the future as much as I possibly can!

We go through life looking for evidence to back up what we have already decided (more on this in Chapter Five). If I decide that I enjoy mixing with new people I will behave differently when I meet them.

The world is unfair. We can all find evidence for that. The world can be horribly unfair and terrible things happen to good people. That said, this is another 'absolute' statement, isn't it? We often feel it, and add strengthening words or phrases to this piece of self-talk that tell us that the world is 'always' unfair, or that bad things happen to us much more than to others. We could equally say the world is a beautiful place and great things happen, and we would be equally right.

I'm not pretending that we can control the world, because we can't. However, what we can, and must control, if we want to change and achieve is how we approach the world around us and how we respond to the things that happen in our lives. We all know stories of people who have been through similar events or had equally troubled childhoods, yet emerged with very different outlooks on life, behaved very differently and achieved very different outcomes.

Thinking the world is unfair, or that you are being singled out for special treatment, means that there is no point in you actually doing anything. We are human, we all suffer, and we are all able to make a difference in our lives and in the lives of others if we decide to. We will look at how we can use self-talk to change our perspective in a moment.

Compared to whom? Here's another favourite pastime for many of us. We love comparing ourselves with other people and these comparisons often find their way into our self-talk. Whenever we compare ourselves with someone else, we seem to do it to prove that they are better than us, or their lives give them advantages that we don't have.

So, what's the answer to this? Stop comparing yourself with others! The only comparison worth making is comparing your current state with your vision for a bigger and better life. And the only reason for making even that comparison is to help you identify what you can do to close that gap and move towards your ideal situation. Compare your actions with your plans, not with other people. That way, you can make a meaningful comparison that leads to positive action, rather than a pointless one that leads to dissatisfaction, resentment or self-pity.

·····························

Self-talk is all a pack of lies. It's just a matter of which set of lies you choose to believe.

·····························

It's all lies! This is the key to our understanding of self-talk: it's all a pack of lies. It's just a matter of which set of lies you choose to believe. As we've seen, self-talk is automatically negative until we are aware of it. Let's look at a few typical examples:

- Nothing I do ever works
- I'm scared of change
- I'm not clever or well educated
- I can't talk in front of groups.

These are all things that people have said to me more than once when asked for examples of their self-talk, so let's start by running them past the 'truth test'. Then try it on some of your own:

- **Nothing I do ever works.** This is a good example of exaggeration and hyperbole. There are two 'absolute' words: 'nothing' and 'ever'. Whenever you use this kind of language it's a sign that you are going well over the top. Have you really got through life and into adulthood without achieving anything at all? Clearly not or you wouldn't be here, so it isn't true, but somehow you've accepted a view of yourself as incapable of achieving anything. This is simply a lie you've told yourself so often that you believe it. If you don't recognise it for what it is and challenge it then it becomes an instruction and you will behave in accordance with it. This means that when faced with a choice you will default to the lowest risk option, doubt your own abilities and reject your own ideas as unworthy and unworkable. At the point of greatest opportunity therefore you will sabotage yourself and the chance will pass you by because you've already decided it will.
- **I'm scared of change.** Even those who most want to change their lives are afraid of change. Change is destabilising, it takes

us out of our comfort zone (see Chapter Two) and makes us feel vulnerable. This statement is just a straightforward expression of that fear, and if we fear something, we will do everything we can to avoid it, so this is another 'instruction' that will lead us to shy away from taking any positive action that may be necessary before we can start our journey towards something different and potentially better than what we have or the situation we are in now.

- **I'm not clever or well educated.** I work with a lot of 'non-traditional' learners – people who didn't achieve well at school and left feeling inferior or stupid, or, as one man put it, that 'I can't learn anything.' If you feel this way, you are putting yourself at a disadvantage compared to others and have a ready-made argument for thinking there is no point in trying. After all, if you're too thick to understand and learn, you might as well not try in the first place. Try expressing an opinion or standing up for yourself when you have low self-esteem and feel inferior to everyone else; it's virtually impossible.
- **I can't talk in front of groups.** The story behind this is one of my favourites. This young man was on the same course as the 'ugly monster' and didn't say a word for two and a half days before I asked him to give an example of his self-talk. Out of nowhere this booming voice almost shouted: 'I can't talk in front of groups!' We all fell about, including him. It was clearly a lie, but one that had prevented him from speaking in groups for as long as he could remember.

So, if you agree that the above statements are not true, why do we believe them and what can we do about it? Exactly; we can tell a positive lie instead, and say it often enough that we believe it and turn it into our new instruction.

Let's take the first of the four statements above – **nothing I do ever works**. We know it's a lie, so why not turn it into a positive lie? How about **everything I do works brilliantly**? Too extreme maybe, and too 'absolute' in its own way, so what about **I can achieve whatever I put my mind to**? Do you think you would shy away from many opportunities if you believed that you could achieve whatever you put your mind to? Neither do I.

I'm scared of change is almost certainly true – most of us are. But are you more scared of change than anyone else? I doubt it. Change happens to us anyway, whether we do anything or not, and a change that we actively seek is much better than one that is done to us. This piece of self-talk casts us a victim, which is not a good place to be. So, let's embrace change: how about **I love change** or **change is exciting and challenging**? This is much better for someone who is looking to improve their life, isn't it? We're telling ourselves to be excited and do something we love. It's putting us in the driving seat.

I'm not clever or well educated can easily become something like **I'm learning all the time** or even better, **I love learning new skills and gaining new knowledge**. You've stopped judging yourself and given yourself permission to learn and grow and take on new experiences.

Finally, you can decide that you **love talking to groups** or that **people are interesting and I enjoy engaging with them**.

Turning these negative statements around is actually good fun and enormously empowering but there are a few 'rules' to consider when changing your self-talk:

- Use the present tense rather than the future – this is stuff you're thinking and doing *now*, not at some undefined time in the future
- Try to fit in some words that show you are engaged and enjoying yourself; words like 'enjoy' or 'love' help to cement the idea of pleasure and positivity that you need to associate with positive action
- Don't be tempted to talk about yourself in the third person: self-talk is personal and immediate, so why distance yourself from it? 'I' is much more powerful than 'you'
- Forget that you don't believe it *right now*, you are making a declaration of intent and you will believe it soon enough

So, stop criticising yourself, stop being scared and start having fun. Come up with some positive self-talk and repeat it as often as you used to repeat the negative old stuff until you believe it. These positive statements are often referred to as affirmations, because you are affirming your chosen truth. We will look at how to turn them into settled habits towards the end of the book (see also pages 184–90).

Henry Ford and the self-fulfilling prophecy

There's a famous quote from Henry Ford and, no, it's not 'any colour you like as long as it's black'. He said a number of other things that are equally memorable and much more helpful. 'If you think you can, or if you think you can't,' said Ford, 'you're right.' What he was saying is that success or failure is a state of mind. If you decide that you can't do something then you will never do it, but if you decide that you can, then you will.

Life isn't quite as simple as that, but there's enough truth in Ford's statement to make it a useful touchstone for a chapter focusing on the power of our thinking and mental attitude to determine our performance. Thinking is not the same as doing, so if we merely *think* we can, it doesn't mean that we will then go out and *do* it. What we can say with confidence is that if we don't even think we can do it, then we most definitely won't.

Things only happen for us if we actually do something to make them happen, but thinking is the precursor to doing. If you look around you now as you are reading, you will see physical things that are only right there in front of you because someone first thought about them. The bench or chair you're sitting on was an idea someone had, the building you're in was designed by an architect, and the light you read by only became possible because someone dreamed that it might be possible to use electricity to power a light bulb. In fact, you are physically sitting where you are right now because of a series of thoughts you had in the past that led you to make the decisions you took that brought you to this version of your here and now.

So, Ford's phrase does us all a favour by putting the responsibility for our thoughts and actions in our own hands. We won't necessarily bring about great results for ourselves, but we can make them much more possible by not giving up before we've started. Excuses, blame, defeatism or self-pity have no place in our thoughts if we want to make our situation better. All they do is confirm for us that we're a victim and that happiness or success are 'not for the likes of us'.

....

What we can and must control if we want to change and achieve is how we approach the world around us and how we respond to the things that happen in our lives.

....

First, we think, and then we do. That was Ford's insight; if we decide we can't do something, then in the act of deciding we rule out a whole host of other possible outcomes. If we decide we can, all those possibilities remain open. Our thoughts become our behaviour, our behaviour leads to actions, and our actions produce our results. Those results, over time, become our lives.

Hopes and fears

Fear. We've spoken about fear already and we will have to talk about it again more than once. All I plan to say about it at this point is that if we avoid taking a risk because of the fear of failure, or the consequences of failure, then we will never get off the starting block. Everything we do that we've never done before carries with it the fear of failure; every step into the unknown comes without a guarantee of success. The only guarantee we can possibly have is that if we *don't* take the occasional chance then we will *never* give ourselves the opportunity to improve our situation.

Let's make a pact at this stage to say that we acknowledge fear exists and that it has its uses, but agree that it has no place in self-improvement beyond reminding us not to take foolish risks. Don't bet your house unless you are prepared to lose it on the journey to your goal; do take the risk of a bruised ego, an affordable financial sacrifice or a bit of discomfort here and there. If you think you can, you're right.

·····························

Success or failure is a state of mind. If you decide that you can't do something then you will never do it, but if you decide that you can, you will.

·····························

Hope is the counterpart of fear

'It's not the despair. I can take the despair. It's the hope I can't stand!' So says John Cleese's hapless head teacher, Brian

Stimpson, in the film *Clockwise*. Hope is necessary in order for us to keep going, but hope is not enough to bring about the result you want. In fact, hope based on nothing very much can be truly devastating when that hope is dashed, and the disappointment of failure can be enough to destroy any chance of future success.

A powerful insight from the business book *Good To Great* by Jim Collins comes from his interview with Major James Stockdale, which led him to describe the Stockdale Paradox. As a prisoner of war in Vietnam for eight years, along with some of his own soldiers, Major Stockdale was in a terrible position with no indication of when their situation would end. Some tried to comfort themselves by making optimistic predictions, such as 'we'll be out by Christmas,' or 'we'll be out by Easter.' While that kept them going until the target date was reached, when they found that their ordeal was still going on long after those target dates had passed some became depressed, or worse. Stockdale told his soldiers that they should do two things that appear at first sight to be contradictory: 1. Expect the worst. 2. Never give up your belief that you will win in the end.

. . . .

Things only happen for us if we actually do something to make them happen.

. . . .

False optimism based on no evidence is just that: it's false. Belief in eventual success, along with acceptance of hardships along the way, enables you to endure and, finally, to achieve. But we are not planning for suffering on a scale remotely like Major Stockdale's; all we need is the knowledge that we have the strength to keep going until we achieve our goals. False hope means that we are setting ourselves up for disappointment. Resilience means that we are determined to succeed and know that we can and will.

The difference between worrying and thinking

Worry is a close relative of fear. All the things that make us fearful are the same as those that cause us to worry. We worry all the time, about almost everything. We worry about upsetting others by telling the truth, so we tell 'white lies' instead. We worry about getting something wrong, so we don't even try to do it. We worry about looking stupid, so we keep our heads down and leave it to others to have a go first. We naturally worry about the people we love and what might happen to them, or about what might happen to us. We worry about money, security, our jobs, our friendships, our health, our age, our appearance, our popularity, our image. With all this worry, how do we ever find the time to actually do anything about any of it?

. . . .

Our thoughts become our behaviour, our behaviour leads to our actions, and our actions produce our results. Those results, over time, become our lives.

. . . .

People often explain away their indecision and delay by saying 'I think too much'; they feel they over-analyse things and take too long to make up their minds to do something. I've said it a number of times about myself in the past and it's almost seen as a badge of honour by some of us: it translates as something like 'I'm so complex and intelligent that I can see both sides of the argument', giving us the perfect excuse to sit and analyse – and procrastinate – to our heart's content.

I now disagree with this entire concept. I don't believe we *can* think too much – thinking is good, thinking produces ideas and plans and motivation, thinking makes things happen. Thinking is positive. What I believe many of us do – in fact, I would say almost all of us – is *worry* too much. Worry is wholly negative. If we worry about something, we build it up into a massive problem; we literally paralyse our ability to think and behave rationally.

····························

If we can't think clearly and we can't make decisions then we can't do anything to deal with the source of our concerns. This is at the heart of our challenge to get out of our own way and build the life we want. Our first act has to be to free ourselves from negative thinking . . .

····························

Worry keeps us exactly where we are. If we spend our time worrying about impending disaster then we are creating a life for ourselves in which disaster is all we will see. If we are worried about money or are uncomfortable in social situations, for example, then we are likely to find that our financial problems or our discomfort increase the more we dwell on our problem.

Dwelling is an interesting concept. It's an Old English word meaning a place to live, so if we dwell on something, it effectively means we are living in it. Do we want to live among our doubts, fears and insecurities? What will happen to us if we do? What would happen if we chose instead to live among our goals and aspirations, thinking about how we could achieve them, and planning what we are going to do to help us work towards them?

If negative self-talk leads to more negativity and positive self-talk leads to more positivity, let's look at some of the practical ways in which our thoughts and behaviours affect concepts such as luck, opportunity and coincidence. We'll confront our ideas on those in Chapter Four.

Self-Talk and the Self-fulfilling Prophecy:
Takeaways from Chapter Three

★ People can help someone who's overweight, but they can't help a monster. That's the power of self-talk

★ **Self-talk is all a pack of lies. It's just a matter of which set of lies you choose to believe**

★ What we can and must control if we want to change and achieve is how we approach the world around us and how we respond to the things that happen in our lives

★ **Success or failure is a state of mind. If you decide that you can't do something then you will never do it, but if you decide you can, then you will**

★ Things only happen for us if we actually do something to make them happen

★ **Our thoughts become our behaviour, our behaviour leads to our actions, and our actions produce our results. Those results, over time, become our lives.**

CHAPTER FOUR

Luck, Opportunity and Coincidence

The lyrics from the great bluesman, Jimmy Witherspoon – lamenting that he wouldn't have any luck at all if it wasn't for the bad kind – sum up how we often react to adverse circumstances in our lives. We blame others, we blame ourselves, and we make the assumption that things are against us. We even decide that somehow we have been singled out for the harshest treatment by fate, or by the universe, as if there is someone or something out there that doesn't like us and wishes us harm. This is a direct result of the most destructive of all habits: the victim mentality.

When things go against us it can genuinely feel like we've been targeted by malevolent forces but we haven't, it's just that something unwelcome has happened and caused us pain or prevented us from doing something we want to do. These incidents can be anything from being overlooked for promotion to losing someone or something special and naturally, they have the power to make us feel bad.

We're allowed to feel bad sometimes; it's part of being human and it can be damaging if we don't allow ourselves to feel down sometimes, or disappointed or angry. We can bemoan our luck and look around for someone to blame if we want to. These feelings are a natural release mechanism and it helps us to express them rather than keep them bottled up; no one is perfect, no one is happy all the time and none of us are above feeling sorry for ourselves from time to time. That said, we should be aware of the danger of staying in that place for so long that it prevents us from seeing things more objectively, dusting ourselves down and moving on.

'Fall down seven times; get up eight times.' *Chinese proverb*

Our brains are excellent at identifying patterns and predicting events and situations. This ability has been essential in our survival as a species, often against enormous odds. We don't think about which shoe we will put on first before we leave home each day, or which direction we need to walk out of the drive; it would be a waste of time and energy to do so. Instead we store information on any number of things and retrieve it instantly for use at the appropriate time. It helps us to function in the world and is efficient and effective. There are some drawbacks to this ability as well and we need to be aware of them so that we can use this innate skill to positive rather than negative effect.

What your brain is doing in creating these patterns is attempting to predict what is about to happen. It does this, and everything else it does, to protect you from harm by identifying risks and removing you from them. Our primary drives are security and fitting in with our fellow humans. By identifying patterns that enable us to predict events we are trying to protect ourselves from unwanted consequences. In effect, we are saying to ourselves: this situation is like all of these previous situations, so it will turn out the same as all the others. Armed with that evidence, we surrender our critical faculties and treat it as another example of what has gone before. It makes sense, except that it is just another version of the self-fulfilling prophecy as, to paraphrase the influential physicist Albert Einstein, if you do the same things every time, you will get the same results.

There is a military saying that generals always fight the previous war: in other words, they know the way their last battle went, so they approach the next one in the same way, assuming it is the same thing. While we don't have to think too much about which shoe to put on first, we may need to think a little more about our next career move, or where we want to live, or what lifestyle we want to lead. If we follow Jimmy Witherspoon's song lyric and decide that the world is against us, we are saying there is no point in trying to do something as we already know it won't work out. Why? Because we are unlucky and bad things always happen to us. That kind of self-talk (see also Chapter Three) leads us to withdraw from the field of battle.

Understanding 'luck'

Let's start with a fundamental question: does luck, good or bad, really exist?

When someone else is successful we often put it down to luck, particularly if they've achieved something we would like to achieve and especially if we don't like them. 'It's not what you know, it's who you know,' we say; or 'They were in the right place at the right time.' We ascribe their success to good fortune or, if we're really resentful, favouritism, nepotism, manipulation and other dark arts. It's not fair; it's typical; it's *wrong*!

This is all very human, all very emotional and all very convenient. Why is it convenient? Because these are things we can do nothing about, so we don't need to do anything. We can content ourselves with raging against the machine and feeling hard done by. This kind of righteous indignation is tempting but achieves nothing. Someone inferior to you has been promoted above you – again. Someone with less talent has been singled out for attention while you slave away, undiscovered. You're right, it isn't fair. The question is, what are you going to do about it?

It seems to me that if someone else has managed to get to know the right people there's a lesson there for me: get to know the right people. If someone else was in the right place at the right time, how did they do it and what's stopping me from doing it too? To which the only correct answer is, me! It's me stopping myself from doing what this other person did. Instead of finding out what I need to do and doing it, I blame luck or build a conspiracy theory.

There are a lot of assertions made by 'lucky' people that there is no such thing as luck. There's the famous Gary Player quote (the great South African golfer who kept winning tournaments by a narrow margin) in which he explained his good fortune by saying: 'You know, I've found that the harder I practise, the luckier I get.' Then there's the oft-quoted statement that 'you make your own luck'. It's a good message.

We are more likely to achieve something if we approach our challenges and opportunities in a positive frame of mind than a negative one; but if we try to pretend that there is no such thing as luck then we are not dealing with the world as it really is. I have already said that bad things happen, that bad stuff happens to good people and good stuff happens to bad people; life can be unfair and suffering is visited on people who by no stretch of the imagination can be said to 'deserve' it.

. . . .

Sometimes, life isn't fair. The question is, what are you going to do about it?

. . . .

So, who is right: Jimmy Witherspoon or Gary Player? They are both right, of course. Luck is real but you can also influence your own outcomes. There are genuine tragedies and they often result from random chance that no one could have predicted, but that doesn't mean we can afford to be fatalistic. Let's examine this further because it is important that we approach this subject with some real clarity and understanding, rather than accepting our fate as an 'unlucky' person or, equally unhelpfully, thinking we can 'wish' ourselves great results. In effect, what we are thinking about here is a core belief that we are likely to be taking with us through the rest of our life.

Can we deal with setbacks or tragedies better than we do?

This is a difficult question, but a very important one. I am not suggesting that we can blithely stroll through life ignoring the inevitable sadness we all experience from time to time. I have had my share of tragedy and loss in life, as most of us have or will have at some time, and I would be a hypocrite if I were to advise you not to let yourself be affected by it.

Reacting to loss with shock, anger and denial is natural and healthy; what sort of person wouldn't feel those emotions at difficult times? It is also essential for our long-term emotional health that we allow ourselves time to process emotions such as grief, loss, anger and even resentment. I think we can even allow ourselves a dose of self-pity when it's called for – we probably deserve it sometimes.

· ·

Being upset by something is not a crime; letting it disrupt the rest of your life is a crime against yourself and everything you are capable of being.

· ·

Being upset by something is not a crime; letting it disrupt the rest of your life is. It's not a crime against anyone else, but it is a crime against yourself. If you allow your setbacks to become permanent then you are denying yourself the opportunity to make something more of your time on earth than you have so far. As we have discussed earlier, you risk going to your grave with your music still inside you.

I have used two words in the introduction to this section: **tragedies** and **setbacks**. They are very different things, but we can easily find ourselves reacting to them as if they were the same. Losing someone you love is a **tragedy**; making a mistake can have tragic consequences. After a tragedy life is never quite the same again, and you are never quite the same person again. However, even in the face of this kind of loss there is a readjustment and even if you are not the same as you were, you can still be a person who experiences happiness, has goals and ambitions, and find yourself laughing again.

A **setback** can seem equally devastating, but while bereavement is permanent, a setback is temporary. A setback is something not going the way we hoped or expected – for example, someone not behaving as we wanted them to, a gamble not paying off, a plan not coming to fruition. If we treat a setback as if it were a tragedy then we devote our energy and passion into denouncing others, claiming the world is unfair and finding reasons to explain our failure to achieve.

Acknowledging our problems is not the same as being defined by them. The world is full of people who have overcome significant setbacks to achieve fulfilment, and those who have come through awful situations to achieve happiness and make a great contribution to the world.

There is a simple formula that illustrates the influence we can have over the events that happen in our lives: $E + R = O$. We are conditioned to think that it is the EVENTS in our lives that determine the OUTCOME ($E = O$). If we think in this way, we have little or no control over events so we have little or no control over outcomes either. However, even in the most negative situation, the ultimate outcome (i.e. how we live our lives from this moment on) is a direct result, not of the event itself, but our RESPONSE to that event. It is the EVENT, and our RESPONSE to it, that produces the OUTCOME. $E + R = O$

Let me give you an example of this. At one time in my career I was facing the possibility (probability – it happened!) of redundancy. My wife, seeing my apparently secure salary disappearing before our eyes and risking the house and our children's security, not unreasonably saw redundancy as a disaster. Her response was to fear it and hope it wouldn't happen. My reaction was completely different: I disliked the job and really wanted to set up my own training business but knew I wouldn't have the courage to walk out and do it. So my response was equally desperate – I wanted to be made redundant so I could go out and achieve my ambition.

Now I'm not discounting the trauma of redundancy or saying it's a good thing: I coached redundant executives a few years ago and for many, it was very bad news. For others, it was as much of a turning point as it was for me. Redundancy often means disaster, but it can mean transformation: E + R = O.

Can we prevent bad things from happening?

We can only make a proper difference in the world if we begin by accepting the world as it really is. Which begs the question, what is that reality? Part of that reality, as we have already seen, is that bad things happen. So the answer to this question would seem at first sight to be obvious: we can't wish the world to be a certain way and we can't do anything to prevent these negative experiences from happening.

This is a book about getting out of our own way, so it is about removing the obstacles that we have put in place ourselves rather than removing those that, depending on our belief system, fate or destiny or the universe puts there for us. In describing E + R = O, for example, I have put forward the view that we can deal with negative experiences by looking on them as an opportunity. We can choose a chance to either use them as confirmation that we are uniquely unfortunate or as a chance to do something different and positive, even in the saddest or most frustrating of circumstances. Preventing bad things from happening at all is a much tougher task but it is worth thinking about whether, and how, we can stop *some* bad things from happening. I believe the things we *can* avoid are those that we ourselves *cause*.

There are things we cannot prevent, as already discussed, but what about the repeating patterns of behaviour that cause some of the bad things in our lives? Actions have consequences, so if our actions cause consequences that we would rather they didn't, could we possibly change those consequences by changing our actions? I think we can, and I think it is imperative for anyone who wants to get better outcomes to look at some of the things we may be doing (or thinking) that cause bad things to happen.

I remember watching a video on a health and safety training course many years ago. It's not a subject that excites most people, but it really should be the most important priority in any workplace or organisation. The video was about accidents and how they happen and if they can be prevented. An accident is often described as an example of 'bad luck' or fate, as if it is out of everyone's control. This video suggested the opposite, as it described a chain of events that led to the accident itself, identifying perhaps seven or eight opportunities to prevent it from happening. These were opportunities that were missed by everyone involved.

The story involved a worker in an engineering factory getting caught in an unguarded machine, with horrific consequences. From memory, some of the links in the chain leading up to the accident were: no guard fitted, no system to record maintenance of the machine (where the lack of a guard would have been noted), lack of awareness of the danger of wearing loose jewellery while operating machinery, lack of training, no automatic cut-off to stop the machine when a foreign object entered it, no reporting or analysis of previous near misses and so on.

If you apply the lessons of that engineering accident to your own life, can you identify patterns of behaviour that increase the risk of injury to, or even destruction of, your hopes and dreams? This is not the pretext for an exercise in self-flagellation; we are looking for the links in the chain leading to our own 'accidents'.

If I review my own life there are a number of characteristic behaviours that have led to some of the 'bad things' including: lack of organisation, indecisiveness, forgetfulness, lack of confidence or self-belief and worrying about what other people think. These have led over the years to any number of negative consequences such as:

- Not applying for a job I wanted because I knew I wouldn't get it
- Being late for important meetings
- Losing an opportunity because I couldn't make a decision
- The death of a much-loved pet
- Allowing myself to be bullied
- Not asking a girl out in case she said 'no'
- Not asking a girl out in case she said 'yes'
- Not achieving what I was capable of achieving.

Many of these behaviours are based on unhelpful habits, which in turn are an expression of unhelpful thoughts, attitudes and beliefs, and we will address this in more detail in Chapter 10. One caveat here, though: don't indulge too much in criticism of yourself for the mistakes of the past, even the recent past. The only value in doing that is to identify these mistakes, learn from them, and work out how you can prevent yourself from making the same mistakes again.

....

Try to avoid going back over past failures and beating yourself up about them. Only review your own life for the purpose of looking forward to what you can do to change things for the better . . .

....

I've given up (most of) these bad habits but, just like you, I am a work in progress. One of the very best habits we can form is to always keep working on ourselves, reminding ourselves what we can do that will help us, and actively doing things that take us closer to our goals. Being a work in progress is so much better than not being a work at all.

Can we cause good things to happen?

There are no guarantees but yes, of course we can. Good things happen randomly in life just as bad things do, and their arrival is always welcome, but we are going to be much more fulfilled if we can cause a few more of those good things to happen as a direct result of our own actions.

. . . .

Actions have consequences, so if our actions cause consequences that we would rather they didn't, we can change those consequences by changing our actions.

. . . .

If you think about the vast majority of the good things in your life they will be there because you did something to bring them about. They will be the result of a decision you made, a phone call, a commitment, a hunch, a plan or an approach to the right person at the right time. You will be able to track almost everything good that you have back to those actions. Think about what would (or wouldn't) have happened if you hadn't taken those actions and whether you would want to deny yourself. We regret the things we didn't do much more than we regret the things we've done.

Opportunity

A well-known definition of luck is 'where opportunity meets preparedness'. We are surrounded by opportunity but if we look the other way we won't see it and will therefore allow it to pass us by. Often we bemoan our lack of opportunity and say things like 'that sort of money isn't for the likes of me' or 'people like us don't have these advantages'. If we think like that, we simply won't notice the opportunities we have.

. . . .

An old technique for training young journalists is to send them off to walk down the local high street for an hour and ask them to come back with at least two stories. The idea is that in order to be a journalist, you need to be able to find the 'story' under the surface of the most ordinary-looking situation. The successful students come back with the human interest story of the founder of an independent shop or a piece of local history. Course tutors are testing their ability to 'sniff out' a story – in other words, an opportunity – and training them to tune in to what's around them.

....

You are in a similar situation to those trainee journalists: you have something you want to do or be and it may be that you need to train yourself to find and act on the opportunities that will help you to be where or who you want to be.

The concept of 'purposeful practice' as described by writers, including Matthew Syed and Malcolm Gladwell, and referenced in my first book *Management Starts With You*, illustrates the importance of preparation in taking advantage of opportunity. In his book *Outliers* Gladwell quotes The Beatles and Bill Gates as examples of people who put in copious amounts of hard work to learn their respective skills, and says that because of that hard work they were then ready to take advantage of the opportunities that came their way. Without that hard work and the learning involved they would not have been able to achieve what they did.

There are countless examples of people with all the natural ability they could ever need but who failed to achieve their potential. It is not always the most talented people who gain the most success, it is often those with the best attitude, the most well-thought-out plan or the greatest commitment. These are the people whose hard work and dedication give them the skills they need to succeed and whose determination provides them with the opportunity to exploit those skills.

British boxer Nicola Adams had ambitions that most people would regard as unachievable, with all the odds stacked against her. From an early age she was driven by the desire to be an Olympic champion. At the time this was impossible, as women's boxing wasn't even an Olympic sport and there seemed to be little possibility of that changing. After winning her first fight at the age of thirteen, she had to wait another four years for the next because there weren't any female opponents for her to compete against. Along the way she encountered racism and sexism too. She is now, of course, a double Olympic champion and has turned professional – in a profession that scarcely existed when she first started working towards it.

. . . .

You are surrounded by opportunity but if you are looking the other way you won't see it and will therefore allow it to pass you by.

. . . .

Opportunities are there for us, often in plain sight, if we could only see them. Nicola Adams spent her adolescence preparing herself for an opportunity that was hardly there at all, but she could see it clearly. When the opportunity finally presented itself she was there, thoroughly prepared, motivated and ready to exploit it.

Coincidences, red Suzukis, yellow Fords and Market Rasen

Do you believe in coincidence? We have all had the experience of thinking about something and suddenly spotting something entirely relevant to what we were thinking. Coincidences happen all the time, whether it's reading a word and then hearing the same word on the radio at the same time, or getting a call from someone we were just thinking about. I've had some weird ones that are hard to explain away, such as playing a Woody Guthrie CD in my car for the first and only time, turning it off and finding that it was apparently still playing: it wasn't, but there happened to be a programme about Woody Guthrie on the radio at that very moment! What are the chances of that? Experiences like these suggest that coincidences are common, but what is a coincidence and does it really tell us anything?

Our brains are receiving countless messages all the time; we are processing or ignoring information every second of the day. Because we can only focus on one thing at a time, we are therefore missing unlimited amounts of information. It's a good thing that we do, as there is no way we could cope with that amount of information and still be able to function, as anyone who has tried to concentrate in a busy office or a noisy household will tell you. The only way we can get anything done or think in any remotely clear-headed and logical way is if we shut out as much of the irrelevant information as we can.

We notice coincidences because they mean something to us. If someone mentions a name or a topic that's important to you then you are likely to tune in to their conversation and take note of what they are saying. Someone playing Woody Guthrie on the radio would have hardly caused a flicker of recognition if I hadn't been listening to him on CD a second before; someone saying 'elephant' at the same time as I was reading the word makes me sit up and take notice but if I hadn't been reading the word at that moment then I wouldn't even have noticed him saying it. We think coincidences are amazing, but we don't register all the non-coincidences.

How might an understanding of coincidence help us to get out of our own way? We notice what we are already 'tuned in' to, so it's worth thinking about what we have alerted our subconscious mind to look out for and tag as relevant and worthy of attention. Let me give you a couple of examples of how coincidence works.

· ·

You notice what you are already 'tuned in' to, so it's worth thinking about what you have alerted your subconscious mind to look out for and bring to your attention.

· ·

I once met someone who lived in Market Rasen, a place in Lincolnshire that I'd never previously heard of, and we spent a few hours talking. When I got home I turned on the radio and the first words I heard were '. . . and here are the racing results from Market Rasen'. On the same afternoon, a place I'd never heard of had cropped up twice in succession. The announcer would have told me about the racing results anyway, but as I have little interest in horse racing and no connections to Market Rasen, I wouldn't even have heard the words. In effect, my brain was saying to me, 'Here's a bit of information that might mean something to you. Up to you what you do with it,' because who knows, Market Rasen may have become important.

If someone in your family buys a certain type of car, say a yellow Ford Focus or a red Suzuki Swift, you start to see those cars everywhere. 'What a coincidence,' you say, 'I keep seeing them everywhere!' Those cars would have been there anyway, but if someone close to you hadn't bought one they would have driven past you completely unnoticed. They have suddenly become important to you, so your brain alerts you to something that may be worth your attention.

This is where goals come in. If you want to be a boxing champion, and you are determined to achieve your goal, you will look for anything that could possibly help you on your way, including training, so that you are in the best possible state to capitalise on it. If your goal is to make money, you will see opportunities for making money everywhere because your brain will have sifted them from all the other information that it sees as irrelevant.

Coincidence can therefore be seen as a message from your brain to tell you that it has been given some information that might help you. Your subconscious mind has noticed something and passed it on to your conscious mind. Once your brain has brought that information to your attention, the rest is up to you.

Focus

I would like to close this chapter with a few words on the importance of focus in making your own luck, making the most of opportunities and creating positive coincidences.

Have you ever noticed how your biggest fears play on your mind, and how many of them actually come true? People often bring about the very thing they are trying hardest to avoid: people who are afraid of being alone end up alone, those who live in fear of running out of money never have enough to live on, people who fear unpopularity end up being unpopular. Why? *Because they are focusing on the wrong thing.*

What you focus on, you get more of. If you focus on fear and negatives you will create more fear and become aware of more negatives. This is sometimes described as having either a scarcity or abundance mentality. Those with a scarcity mentality are constantly worried that they don't have enough of whatever they need; whether money, time, friends or energy, they are focusing on what they lack and worrying that they will never have what they need. When opportunities present themselves, as they always will, someone with scarcity mentality won't even notice them, or will come up with reasons not to act on any they do notice. They are, quite literally, getting in their own way to the extent that they can't see what's available to them.

Those with an abundance mentality know that there is opportunity out there and that they can go and find it. The knowledge that there is always something they can do to help themselves gives them the confidence to take action. If they try something that doesn't work as well as they hoped, they think, 'Well, let's find out why, learn from it and try something different.' Scarcity mentality makes you worry and creates more scarcity, while abundance mentality makes you look for solutions and try them. Perhaps you really can make your own luck.

Luck, Opportunity and Coincidence:
Takeaways from Chapter Four

★ Sometimes, life isn't fair. The question is, what are you going to do about it?

★ **Being upset by something is not a crime, letting it disrupt the rest of your life is a crime against yourself and everything you are capable of being**

★ Actions have consequences, so if our actions cause consequences that we would rather they didn't, we can change those consequences by changing our actions

★ **You are surrounded by opportunity but if you are looking the other way then you won't see it and will therefore allow it to pass you by**

★ You notice what you are already 'tuned in' to, so it's worth thinking about what you have alerted your subconscious mind to look out for and bring to your attention

★ **Avoid going back over past failures and beating yourself up about them. Only review your own life for the purpose of looking forward to what you can do to change things for the better.**

CHAPTER FIVE

Listen, Or Your Tongue Will Make You Deaf

I'm against tuition fees for higher education. I feel that the student loan system in the UK loads young people with debt, makes money an issue in education when it should be about ability, and it is completely unfair and wrong. When fees were introduced in 1998, and increased further in 1992, I confidently predicted that numbers of university applications would fall. So when I saw a newspaper article with a headline proving that the number of university applications had in fact gone up, what do you think I did? Did I read it with interest and an open mind, consider the facts and change my mind accordingly? No, of course not – I hurriedly turned the page so I wouldn't have to think about it.

Why did I do that? Why would I not even consider another point of view? Why did I deny the evidence that was presented to me? The answer is, of course, that by not reading the article I could carry on holding my existing opinion without troubling myself with any facts that might get in the way of it. Tuition fees are bad, they put people off going to university. Even if, in fact, they don't.

This is an example of cognitive dissonance, a psychological term describing the discomfort of holding two contradictory views at the same time, or being confronted by views that conflict with our own certainties. We want to believe that we are logical, but in reality we are nothing of the kind: we are driven by our emotions. My aversion to tuition fees is an emotional one based on my background and personal history; it is not the result of considered research and analysis. In effect, I am against tuition fees because I am against them.

....

We want to believe that we are logical, but in reality we are nothing of the kind. We are driven by our emotions.

....

This is why we buy newspapers that express opinions we already agree with, so we can confirm our own prejudices and be comforted by how clever and right we are. It's why we make friends with like-minded people. It's also why we tend to enjoy complaining about bosses, colleagues, governments, neighbours, foreigners and others as it enables us to feel part of something and to be vindicated by being right.

This is all natural and in many ways perfectly harmless. We think what we think, believe what we believe, and look for evidence that proves us right. This behaviour allows us to form social bonds with others, fit into our various social and work environments and form our own world view. These are all good things, so is there a problem with any of that? Actually, yes, there is, and I believe that some of these problems are fundamental to the biggest problem of all: our tendency to prevent ourselves from moving forward, taking on new information and letting go of unhelpful and unfounded beliefs.

If we only listen to ourselves, or to pre-selected sources of information, we will never hear anything to challenge our existing beliefs. This means we will never change. We could go through our entire life believing something that is incorrect, self-limiting or damaging and in doing so prevent ourselves from seeing or taking an opportunity that could be of real value to us. I don't feel I am hurting myself or anyone else by opposing university tuition fees, but what if my belief was one that prevented me from doing something positive?

....

If we only listen to ourselves, or to pre-selected sources of information, we will never hear anything to challenge our existing beliefs. This means we will never change.

....

This chapter will examine the ways in which we sabotage ourselves simply through this inability to take on new information or to make decisions based on facts rather than prejudice. We will look at how this can stop us from seeing things as they really are instead of how we perceive them to be, and how much simpler it is to make decisions, assess risks and commit to doing things if we unlock our protective doors and let in some fresh air.

Pride or prejudice?

We are so wedded to a particular world view that we automatically reject anything that doesn't fit in with it, or that makes us feel uncomfortable. As far as we are concerned if we can't accept or make sense of something without compromising our belief system then it can't be right and has to be dismissed. This is one reason why it can be so hard for other people to help or advise us; because we either don't want to or are incapable of accepting what they tell us. There is the added complication that they will be giving you advice based on their opinions, so what you are getting is their world view. Their advice is coming from their own perspective and they may therefore not understand yours, which is likely to end with mutual misunderstanding and miscommunication. Each time this happens you are strengthened in your view that other people don't understand you and their advice is wrong – excellent reasons for staying where you are and carrying on as before.

The reasons for or justification of our prejudices may not be valid but they are experienced by the holder of a prejudice as if they are unshakeable tenets to live by. Everything a prejudiced person faces can be explained or understood in the terms of that prejudice. So, why is prejudice such a common human response?

On a practical level prejudice makes a lot of sense. It saves us from having to analyse everything before making a decision, means that we can make assumptions and act on them quickly and helps us to understand the world around us. In fact the human brain looks for patterns for two very good reasons.

Firstly, patterns give us predictability so we can pick up on signals and know what is going to happen next, which is very useful for us as we deal with everyday life. It saves time and increases our feeling of security. This is why we hold on to opinions that are out of date and irrelevant, and why we stay in comfort zones long after they have stopped being comfortable: we like predictability because we mistake it for security.

. . . .

This is why we hold on to opinions that are out of date and irrelevant, and why we stay in comfort zones long after they have stopped being comfortable: we like predictability because we mistake it for security.

. . . .

Secondly, if we recognise patterns and know what we should normally expect to see or experience, it makes it easier for us to identify anything different or unexpected. We can then be on our guard and successfully avoid it or fight it off.

These are instinctive skills but they are not always appropriate to our needs if we are looking to change and grow. In fact they are defensive techniques, designed to protect us from external threats; they are not designed to help us identify opportunity or embrace the new and difficult.

· ·

In defending ourselves so successfully against risk and danger that we never challenge our core beliefs, we are also protecting ourselves against the possibility of change and growth.

· ·

We like to be right and dislike being wrong. It's why we reject advice and also in part why we like to give advice to others. We need to be right, because being wrong is difficult for us to accept. Being right confirms us in our current world view and means that we don't need to change anything. Being wrong means that if I'm wrong about one thing then I could be wrong about other things too, and so I will doubt myself and wonder whether anything I believe is really true at all. Instead of accepting that in a spirit of intellectual curiosity we pull down the shutters until the risk of exposure has gone. Even the most liberal and well-meaning of us don't really like anyone to challenge our understanding or opinions. It's a mixture of pride and prejudice that we need to deal with if we are going to get out of our own way.

Challenging your beliefs and attitudes

How do we challenge our core beliefs without throwing ourselves into doubt and uncertainty? One answer to that is another question: what's so wrong with doubt and uncertainty? If we are so entrenched in our current way of thinking that we can't ever change it, how will we ever learn anything new? A little doubt and uncertainty can be good for us if it causes us to reflect on what we are doing and the results our behaviour is producing. What once worked may not work next time and what has never worked at all is probably worth re-evaluating.

Another answer is that challenging ourselves does not mean that we are fighting a battle we must either win or lose. Many of us are in the habit of conflating one thing with another, so we think that if we challenge a particular fact or belief then it means we are challenging ourselves. If we think that way then we perceive the challenge itself to be a threat and will defend ourselves vigorously against it.

Defending ourselves against a perceived threat can be done in one of two ways: we either come out fighting and don't give the other view a chance, or we allow ourselves to be thrown into doubt and insecurity, and ultimately to be defeated. If one of your opinions is proved to be wrong, it doesn't mean that *you* are wrong. If an idea you have doesn't work, it doesn't mean that *you* don't work. If you've been wrong in the past, it doesn't mean that you will be wrong again in the future, and if you are wrong about one thing, it doesn't mean you are wrong about everything.

As we saw earlier in Chapter Three on self-talk, our attitudes and opinions form the instructions we give to ourselves, and these instructions directly impact on what we decide to do. If we don't challenge those beliefs then we will carry on acting them out. Is this a problem? That depends on the nature of those beliefs. If our beliefs are negative ones that disempower us and make us avoid trying anything new, making a decision or committing to something, then yes, it's a problem.

Assumptions are a real issue for most of us. We make assumptions because we prejudge a person or situation based on similar people or situations. If it looks like something else we've already seen and categorised then we decide that the new will be the same as the old. On one level this is sensible; after all, why waste time doing something that you've failed at before? On another level it's just an example of lazy thinking.

The risk with making assumptions is that we will feel there is no point in doing something if we have already decided what the outcome will be. If you listen carefully, you will hear examples of this everywhere.

I ran a programme for long-term unemployed people and began the first session by asking them to identify the reasons why they couldn't find work. It wasn't a very positive first few minutes as we easily filled a piece of flipchart with all their barriers. Some even admitted afterwards that they had quite enjoyed being given the opportunity to vent and complain. When we summarised the barriers we found that many of them were assumptions and while they may well have been based on experience, it showed how easy it is to generalise based on one or two experiences and come up with a set of 'rules' that we think apply across the board.

· ·

It is easy to generalise based on one or two experiences and come up with a set of 'rules' that we think apply across the board: the 'assumptions' we make as a result get in the way of reality.

· ·

I remember the summing-up from that session going something like this: we can't get jobs because we're too young/too old/too highly qualified/not qualified enough/too experienced/too inexperienced. Amid the smiles of recognition we decided that it would be more positive for the group if we abandoned these assumptions and worked on things we could affect instead. I understand the difficulties of unemployment, and have experienced them myself, but without that shift in attitude it would have been hard to motivate the group to believe that it was possible to get work. Most of them did.

If it ain't broke, don't fix it is a popular concept. It is also a good excuse not to try to improve on what you already have. There's no point in fixing something that's working well if all you are going to do is replace it with something that works no better, and some people do waste a lot of their time 'fiddling' around to no purpose. Change for the sake of change is often an excuse to shuffle the deckchairs on the *Titanic*.

Things don't have to be 'broke' to need fixing. They must be no longer fit for purpose, not relevant to what you really want to do or producing predictable but average results. Jim Collins starts his book *Good To Great* with the phrase 'Good is the enemy of great'. Challenging yourself will involve deciding if the routines you have are working well enough for you not to need to change them.

· ·

Things don't have to be 'broke' to need fixing. They must be no longer fit for purpose, not relevant to what you really want to do or producing predictable but average results.

· ·

The true test is whether what you are currently doing is producing results you are happy with. If it is, then it isn't broke and doesn't need fixing. If, however, your current attitudes and behaviours aren't producing the results you want then it may well be a good idea to fix them. This book has many techniques and approaches you can use to 'fix' broken patterns of thought and behaviour.

The art of listening

Most of us are pretty shocking when it comes to listening. (Many of us aren't great at talking honestly and openly either, but listening is the most powerful communication skill.) 'Listen or your tongue will make you deaf' is a powerful statement first recorded by George Bernard Shaw and attributed to a Cherokee chief. The message is that all the time we're talking we are simply repeating what we already think we know, but if we listen to other people there is always the chance that we might learn something.

Listening is powerful for a number of reasons, some of which may surprise you:

People like to be listened to. I would go further still and say that people *need* to be listened to. It's hard to underestimate the power of listening as a means of making another person feel valued. When you meet someone new they will want to talk about things that are important to them – their family, their job, their experiences. The most important person in the world to you is, if you're totally honest, you. Your family too, of course, but they make up your world and are extensions of you. You see the world through your eyes, experience life through your own perceptions and relate to others through the filter of your values, beliefs and the experiences and prejudices that create your likes and dislikes. If someone honours those things by listening to you then you will feel validated because someone else is showing an interest in you and your place in the world.

In the famous Tony Hancock television sketch, 'The Blood Donor', Hancock is talking to a man (played by Hugh Lloyd) while they wait to give blood. Hancock talks endlessly about himself and gives his views on blood donation and anything else he can think of. Hugh Lloyd's contribution is to simply say: 'Yes', 'Oh, I agree!',

'You're right'. As Lloyd leaves, Hancock says: 'What a nice man, what a really nice man.'

In the modern age, if you take a look at a social media site such as LinkedIn, count the number of comments to posts that simply say 'So true'. In many ways the poster of these articles is doing it to get as many 'So trues' as they can, and many of us eagerly scroll through our phones to see how many 'likes' we get for our posts. Digitally or in person, we crave relevance and recognition.

. . . .

I was working on an archaeological dig many years ago as a summer job/holiday and found myself working on the side of a hill next to another young man. For four hours he talked about his problems with his girlfriend and other aspects of his life, confiding all sorts of problems and dilemmas he was going through. All I said in the course of those four hours was Hugh Lloyd-esque things like, 'yes', 'of course', 'oh', 'mmm' and a number of other wordless listening noises. I don't remember being asked for, or offering an opinion on anything he said. He didn't want opinions or suggestions, he wanted to be listened to. At the end of the afternoon he shook my hand and said: 'Thanks for all your advice.'

. . . .

Listening builds better relationships than talking ever does. Of course we must talk, but if we listen first then it helps us both.

If you don't listen to someone else how do you know whether they have any interest whatsoever in what you are talking about? No one likes being the victim of a monologue delivered by someone who is only interested in themselves, and most of us will politely find a way to extricate ourselves as quickly as we politely can.

In his book *Outliers* Malcolm Gladwell points to several case studies of people with all the natural ability to succeed in life, but who lack the social skills and confidence to ask for what they want, or to make the adjustments they need to make to their behaviour to get a crucial decision-maker onside. This is often a confidence issue based perhaps on class or education. If you are going to enlist the help of another person, even if that includes saying things they don't want to hear, listening to them first is a very good way of overcoming barriers, real or perceived, and creating the essential rapport both parties need to make a transaction work. In particular, people love it if you've met them once and then when you meet them again you allude to something from your previous conversation. It makes them feel important and much more well-disposed towards you. This isn't manipulation, this is influencing. Why not show that you remember someone and value what they said?

....

If you listen to someone they are much more likely to listen to you.

....

If you listen to someone they are much more likely to listen to you. Listening is not a passive thing. The phrase 'active listening' is often used to describe the process of being actively engaged in what the other person is saying to you. We can show that we are listening in a number of ways. Here are a few simple things we can do that show we are genuinely interested:

- **Repeat key phrases back to them.** Called 'reflecting', this enables the other person to realise not only have they been listened to but they have also been *understood*. Being understood is crucial as it's the first step towards genuine two-way communication. We don't need to robotically repeat their words, but framing a reflective question is a great way to put a full stop on a topic – for example, you could say, 'So you feel that you've been unfairly treated?' or 'You said that money is important to you, is that right?' If they say, 'Yes, that's right,' you've secured agreement on the nature of the issue, even if you haven't yet resolved it.

- **Ask questions.** Questions are great! All conversations are a mix of question and answer. Here, the key thing for a skilled listener is to ask questions that develop what the other person has just said. The great interviewers listen to what people say to them and ask something relevant to what they've just said: the less skilful or confident interviewers keep quiet while the other person is speaking then ask the next question from their prepared list. This shows that they weren't paying attention and are less interested in the interviewee than they are in themselves. This is a key behaviour and can make all the difference between the greats such as Parkinson and the rest, and between you being able to establish genuine rapport with someone or making them feel you are not paying attention to them. Good questions draw people out so they open up, and draw them in so they want to engage with you.

- **Be patient.** Don't rush to have your say or give your opinion first. Chances are it won't be listened to anyway! Once you have heard the other person out you can say your piece, hopefully in a more appropriate way than you would have done by steaming straight in. If you pause and take stock of what they have said before piling in yourself you may learn something from them – after all, you already know what you think, don't you?

  If the other person knows that you have listened to them properly and understood them, they don't need to keep repeating themselves, and they are now free to listen to you. For most people, even the most talkative and self-centred, simple politeness and fair play dictates that they can now listen to you.

- **Listening is less stressful than speaking.** We're not all full of confidence and some of us find talking to strangers or speaking in public stressful. The most seasoned networkers among us will have things going on in their lives that affect how they feel, and sometimes even they will have times when it is all a bit too much of an effort to keep 'performing' and pushing themselves forward. Even when you need to tell people about yourself and your plans and ideas, treat yourself to asking a few questions and letting someone else do the talking. You will probably find that by the time it's your turn it will feel more natural.

Why should you care about how others perceive you and your communication skills? This book isn't about everyone else, it's about you and your ability to feel more fulfilled and build the life you want. Building that life is, of course, up to you, but it isn't a solo activity. In making the changes you want to make, and attracting the opportunities you are interested in, you will need to deal with others, to influence them and to relate to them.

- **Listening is essential to learning and growth** so listen to some of the wisdom of the ages and follow some of these ideas:

....

'Seek first to understand, then to be understood.'
Dr. Stephen R. Covey, author of the bestselling
7 Habits of Highly Effective People

'Better to be quiet and have people think you're a fool than to open your mouth and prove that you are one.'
Mark Twain

'You've got two ears and one mouth: use them in that proportion' *My science teacher*

'Listen or your tongue will make you deaf.' Cherokee saying

'While you're talking, you are not learning anything. You are simply repeating what you already think you know' Alan Hester

....

Listen, Or Your Tongue Will Make You Deaf:
Takeaways from Chapter Five

★ We want to believe that we are logical, but in reality we are nothing of the kind. We are driven by our emotions

★ **If we only listen to ourselves, or to pre-selected sources of information, we will never hear anything to challenge our existing beliefs. This means we will never change**

★ We hold onto opinions that are out of date and irrelevant, and we stay in comfort zones long after they have stopped being comfortable. We like predictability because we mistake it for security

★ **It is easy to generalise based on one or two experiences and come up with a set of 'rules' that we think apply across the board: the 'assumptions' we make as a result get in the way of reality**

★ Things don't have to be 'broke' to need fixing. They must be no longer fit for purpose, not relevant to what you really want to do or producing predictable but average results

★ **If you listen to someone they are much more likely to listen to you.**

CHAPTER SIX

How Many Ways Do I Love Me? Self-esteem and Confidence

· ·

As a new undergraduate in my first term at university I was leaving the room at the end of a tutorial when the tutor called me back and asked me to sit down. He wanted to talk about my essay. This was the first essay I had written in my first term. I naturally assumed it was bad news. 'I've been reading your essay,' he said, 'and I have to say that this is the best essay by a first-year undergraduate that I have ever read.' It was very nice to hear, of course, and quite a relief, but before I had reached the end of the corridor I thought, 'Well, that was great, but I won't be able to write another one like that!'

· ·

Of all the different methods of getting in your own way that we deal with in the course of this book the most important one is almost certainly a lack of self-belief and, what goes hand in hand with it, a lack of confidence. It doesn't matter what other people say in order to convince you that you are special or talented and have as much right to happiness as anyone else; it only has an impact once you yourself start to believe it.

Too many of us simply do not feel that we are good enough to succeed; we don't believe in ourselves, our skills or our ambitions. Because we don't believe in ourselves, we take each setback as evidence that we somehow don't deserve to achieve our dreams, that we are somehow getting above our station in attempting to achieve something for ourselves. Without that core self-belief we don't have the commitment necessary to overcome obstacles and see the thing through.

There are two lines in the hymn 'All Things Bright And Beautiful' that irritated me from a very early age (actually, they made me angry, but why do we insist on hiding behind these lesser emotions?). Those lines are: '*The rich man at his castle, the poor man at his gate/God made them high or lowly, and ordered their estate.*' This sums up a whole attitude to life and society and social mobility that should be well and truly a thing of the past. We don't have a pre-ordained level that we should accept and never try to get out of, whether it's based on economics, class, education or anything else.

In my career as a trainer I have worked with many people who have entered my classes with the self-defeating view that they are stupid, or that life has already passed them by and they are wasting my time and theirs by trying to improve their lives. One man in his forties even said that he didn't think he was capable of learning anything because he had been labelled stupid at school as a result of undiagnosed dyslexia: together, we achieved so much that he won an Adult Learner of the Year award and made a speech of acceptance in front of more than a hundred people. That potential was always in him but it could only start to be realised once he started to believe in himself and all the possibilities he was opening up as he began to enjoy the process of learning and achieving.

. . . .

Asking the question 'What if I'm not good enough?' pretty much guarantees the answer that you're not. So don't ask it!

. . . .

My insecurity as a young undergraduate was partly based on my working-class background but even more on my tendency to compare myself with others (more of which in the next chapter). I was only the second person from my village to go to university (my sister was the first) and faced with the thousands of other students I naturally assumed I shouldn't really be there and it would only be a matter of time until I was found out. This fear of exposure is a common one and is behind an awful lot of our reluctance to get out there and do whatever it is we really want to do. Asking the question 'What if I'm not good enough?' pretty much guarantees the answer that you're not. So don't ask it!

What is self-esteem and how do I create it?

Self-esteem is, quite simply, what we think of ourselves. Our level of self-esteem directly impacts on our self-confidence, so the higher our self-belief, the easier it is to behave in a way that demonstrates our ability to be significant and command the respect and attention of others.

Self-esteem is fragile and easily undermined. A lot of us can point to a simple phrase or comment made by someone that has stayed with us for years and entered our psyche as an unchallenged truth. This can be someone showing their faith in you as a person or in your ability, or it can be the complete opposite. Even the most casual remark uttered by someone who may not even have been particularly important to you can be the one that stays with you; a comment on your appearance perhaps, or a prediction about your future. The comment may even come from someone who didn't know you well enough to be qualified to make that judgement, but there it is, burned into your memory.

Can we rely on others to bolster our self-esteem for us? Not really, although of course it's always nice if people do. The task of building your own self-esteem is, in reality, a task for you and no one else. So what are the magic tools for making you feel better about yourself?

I used the word 'significant' just now and this is an important concept in self-esteem. Most of the ways in which we can improve our self-esteem, i.e. feel better about ourselves, are through doing things that enhance our feeling of being significant or influential in some way. First, we need to feel significant in our own lives. Then, and only then, can we feel significant in the lives of others. Let's look at these two sides of the coin.

Being significant in your own life is essential to your self-esteem. It's the building block of self-belief. It is also more complicated than it sounds because it is easy to get the balance wrong. We can either make ourselves too important or not important enough. Chapter Seven will deal in detail with the idea that we can cause real damage to our happiness by making ourselves too important and thinking that everyone is interested in criticising us and putting us down. Equally common is not taking our needs and wants seriously enough and forgetting to work on, or reward, ourselves.

. . . .

We need to feel significant in our own lives. Then, and only then, can we feel significant in the lives of others.

. . . .

If we work out (more accurately, recognise) what is significant to us and spend more of our time doing it then we will feel better. But if we deny ourselves that significance we will feel frustrated. Frustration can lead to bitterness and anger, then to blame and self-blame; these are all emotions that harm us and turning them on ourselves or others makes us feel worse.

Self-esteem is not arrogance or vainglory but recognition that we are doing things that mean something to us. We feel better about ourselves more for what we do than for what we are. Self-esteem grows through taking action that leads to significant results. We can build our self-esteem in a variety of ways, all of them positive actions. Here are a few examples of this:

- **Achievement.** Setting ourselves a goal and achieving it. Whether it's having a difficult conversation with someone, running a half-marathon (or a mile), writing a book or being top performer in your team there is no better feeling than setting out to do something and doing it.
- **Celebration.** Achieving something is its own reward, but it is even better if you acknowledge it by celebrating in some way. If you set yourself a target and fail to acknowledge your achievement then there is less incentive to work hard to achieve the next one.
- **Rewarding the right behaviour.** This works with small goals and rewards as well as bigger ones. When I first went self-employed I had a list of people to phone. I didn't want to do it and would find any excuse not to do so. Soon I discovered that having a coffee *after* I had phoned five people was a much better feeling than having it *instead of* phoning them: I felt I deserved it!
- **Learning.** The satisfaction of learning a new skill is hard to beat. Whether it's a new language, a new guitar chord or a new craft, the feeling of mastering something you couldn't

previously do is a great boost to your self-esteem. It's one thing to say, 'I would like to . . .' but it's another thing altogether to be able to say, 'I've done it.'

- **Responsibility.** This is a word some people shy away from, but the more we realise that we are responsible for where we are now and what happens in the future, the more responsibility we will be able to take. Taking responsibility means we take the power that goes with it; if we act with purpose, we will take control.

Every time you do something that takes you forwards you feel better; every time you don't you will feel worse. If you avoid doing something because it's difficult or scary then the next time you face a similar challenge it will be even more difficult and even scarier. Do it and you open up all the possibilities listed above. If you achieve it you'll feel great; if you celebrate, you'll show it was worth achieving. If you reward yourself for trying then you will want to try again. If you achieve a particular challenge then great, but if you don't you will still learn from it and can apply your learning to the next effort you make. By taking responsibility for your life you will take control of your actions and feel that your life is meaningful.

· ·

Every time you do something that takes you forwards you feel better; every time you don't you will feel worse.

· ·

Viktor E. Frankl, who survived the Nazi concentration camps, called his great book *Man's Search for Meaning*. In our humble way, we need to find our own meaning; there has to be more. Most of us already know what that is, but we neglect ourselves. Stop looking the other way.

. . . .

I was a senior manager in a company and spent some time with a business coach (how indulgent!). At the end of an hour of talking about all the issues the company was facing and how I was working to resolve them, he waited for me to stop talking. Then he said: 'I don't see you in there. You've spent an hour talking about everyone else and what they need but you haven't mentioned yourself once. What do *you* need?' I hadn't thought about that at all.

. . . .

Being significant in the lives of others is what really turbocharges your self-esteem. Self-esteem fuels confidence and confidence fuels motivation. If you know that you are making a difference to someone else's life your own sense of significance improves in turn. We are motivated to the extent that we have something to aim for and a desire to do it, and when that something impacts positively on others we feel worthwhile and want to keep on doing it. Right at the top of most people's personal motivators is the desire to 'make a difference'. We need to feel that because we are here, as a direct result of our actions and our influence we have made a positive contribution to our family, friends or work colleagues. If they recognise that difference, and thank us for it, all the better, but it is its own reward anyway.

This is reciprocal altruism. I do something that makes you feel better and in return I feel better for having done it. There's no shame in that and it doesn't mean that there is no such thing as an unselfish act; it does mean that there is such a thing as a 'win-win' and let's have as many of those as we can. No good deed goes unrewarded in the world of self-esteem.

We all want to have a positive impact on those around us but how best can we do that and is it really necessary for our own self-esteem?

- **You make your biggest impact when you are truest to yourself.** Don't worry about others thinking you're being selfish for following your own interests and ambitions. Of course if you have responsibilities you need to make sure you don't neglect them but that doesn't mean neglecting yourself. If you express yourself as fully as you can and make things happen then it can only be good for you and everyone else. You're here to make the most of your own life, not to live anyone else's life.
- **Be you.** Don't try to be someone else, you won't be very good at it. Be the best version of you and you will do so much better than being a poor version of someone else.
- **Get involved.** If you need to meet people in order to learn something or gain introductions to the right people, then do it.

Make the time to talk to people, to ask questions and to get to know them.

- **Plan ahead.** At work you probably take it for granted that you have a 'to do' list. You have appraisals and one-to-ones with your manager where you agree goals and objectives, which become your targets for the year, quarter or week ahead. Everyone considers these to be necessary to ensure that you get things done, but very few of us carry the same disciplines into our home and personal lives. I know you don't want your life outside work to be the same as your working days, but if something is important to you why not put a plan together with some actions to take? If you don't plan, you don't prepare, and if you don't prepare then you won't have the resources or the focus you need to get anything done.

- **Just do it.** If you do something, then something will happen. If you don't do anything, then nothing ever will. Even worse, as we saw in Chapter One (page 7), not doing anything means that if something else happens, we will have no control over it. Therefore, doing nothing means that something else will happen, and it may not be welcome. The American self-help author Jack Canfield (*The Success Principles*) has a mantra for this: 'Oh what the heck? Go for it anyway!'

- **Review it.** If you take action and it doesn't produce the results you want, review your own actions and try something else. Look for evidence, not opinion: what works and what doesn't work? If it doesn't work, change it or stop doing it; if it does work, do it, or at least a version of it, again.

We respond to what the world shows us but what the world shows us depends on what we generate ourselves. Think Market Rasen and Suzuki Swifts (page 76). Put out a message that you mean business and the world (through your brain) will show you what you need to see.

....

Just do it. If you do something, then something will happen. If you don't do anything, then nothing will.

....

Dealing with criticism and negative feedback

Sportsmen and women interviewed after a triumphant performance will often say things like: 'I wanted to prove people wrong'. They are able to turn the negative opinions of others into a piece of motivational self-talk so that proving people wrong becomes a goal in itself. It hasn't really, but they have turned it into another tool to help them achieve, rather than an excuse for not doing so.

We don't enjoy being criticised. It can be painful and our first instinct is to defend ourselves against it. We defend ourselves in one of two ways: either we attack the 'attacker' or we cave in and accept that we deserve it. Neither of these is effective: yes, they will make the critic go away either as a winner or loser, but they won't help us.

If you are a sensitive soul (and most of us are) then you will naturally avoid criticism if you can. One of the most effective ways

111

we avoid this is not to do anything to bring it on ourselves. Often this means not stepping out of our comfort zone and taking a risk. Other negative behaviours we may be tempted into include hiding our mistakes from others for fear of feeling embarrassed or awkward. This goes against everything we need to do if we want to change or improve or achieve anything more than we are currently achieving.

....

Let's all accept one important truth, which will make our lives a whole lot easier. We are not perfect, you are not perfect. You cannot do something new and get it right first time every time; it just will not happen. You will make mistakes, you will feel guilt and you will sometimes look stupid. You need to train that troublesome ego of yours to accept this truth. Then relax.

....

There are two types of criticism: useful and useless. Some criticism comes from people who don't know what they're talking about, so believing their criticism is not particularly sensible. Some people like to give advice whether or not they know anything to base it on. Whether criticism is meant well or not, whether it is well informed or not, it's up to you what you do with it.

Criticism is just someone's way of giving you feedback. Feedback is good – companies pay huge sums of money in order to get feedback from their customers. They do this for several reasons, all of which apply to you as a person. Feedback gives them:

- Information on what their customers and potential customers (other people) think, how they behave and why
- An independent assessment of their image and reputation, how they are seen and how people relate to them
- Positive messages they can relay to others to establish their credibility as an organisation
- Areas where they can improve on their current performance
- Opportunities for further business development.

Could you make use of feedback from friends, colleagues, family and people who know what they are talking about in the field you want to achieve in? Hard as you may find it, try to treat feedback (a nicer word than criticism) as if was offered in a spirit of generosity and support, then take from it the useful advice that will help you to refine your behaviour so it is more likely to produce the results you want. And if the feedback is ignorant or useless thank them anyway . . . and then prove them wrong.

How do I find confidence . . . and keep it?

Confidence is a notoriously fragile thing. It depends on self-esteem. If you believe in yourself and what you have to offer the world then you will behave with confidence. If you don't, it's difficult. The best and most satisfying way to build your confidence therefore is to build your self-esteem. Even if you don't currently have much faith in yourself I hope that some of the advice in this chapter will help you to develop some more. This is an area in which every step we take is important and helps us to overcome our barriers to achievement or a better life.

· ·

Real and sustainable confidence is built on evidence of achievement.

· ·

In addition to the pointers already given in this chapter for improving your self-esteem, here are a few habits it's worth getting into if you want to build your self-confidence – and who doesn't? Lack of confidence is the biggest single barrier to living the life you are capable of, and the number one reason for getting in your own way.

Forgive yourself. We all get things wrong, so don't dwell on past mistakes. Look back by all means, but only for the purpose of looking forward. Remember, you did what you did because it was the best you were capable of at that time of your life; you didn't do it wrong because you wanted to. Learn from it and put in place whatever you need (research, attitude or resources) to do better next time.

Be logical, not emotional. When I find myself in a situation I don't want to be in, I ask myself, what did I do to allow this to happen? (*Actually*, I feel sorry for myself for a while first, and then do the sensible and productive thing once I've had my little self-indulgent moment – I'm only human!). Analyse it, decide on the solution and carry it through.

Act as if you're confident . If you wish you were more confident then *be* more confident. Wishing is pointless and confirms you in your current state as a victim of circumstance or fate. It is entirely possible to 'act' yourself into a more confident state of mind simply by behaving as if you were already confident. Ask yourself what a confident person would do in a given situation and do it. If you think this is impractical then think of a time when you had to do something you didn't want to do and did it anyway. Once you're doing it, whatever happens, you're doing it.

Focus on them, not you. Don't think about yourself, think about them. What's important to the people you are dealing with? They are more interested in their own concerns than yours. Much more on this in the next chapter.

Prepare. Get ready! I used to do sales meetings with a colleague. He was a great salesman and was always as well prepared as he could be. As we got out of the car and put on our jackets, he would say, 'Right, boys, armour on!' He was prepared for the meeting and his preparation covered knowledge, attitude and a suit jacket.

Confidence is easily undermined by our own self-talk, by criticism from others and through our past experience of trying something and failing. As we saw in Chapter Two (Your Brain: A User's

Guide, pp25–40) our lack of self-esteem, and therefore confidence, can stem from the messages we received from our parents or other role models, or from our experiences at school. If we're told something often enough, we tend to believe it, and we then reinforce it by telling it to ourselves. At its worst our lack of confidence may not allow us to try at all because we don't believe we are capable of succeeding.

Remember, confidence is a state of mind, and if we are to get out of our own way then we need to start controlling the instructions we give ourselves. The more we try and the more we learn, improve and eventually succeed, the more evidence we are building of achievement and capability. Real and sustainable confidence is built on creating that body of evidence.

How Many Ways Do I Love Me? Self-esteem and Confidence: **Takeaways** from Chapter Six

★ Asking the question 'What if I'm not good enough?' pretty much guarantees the answer that you're not. So don't ask it!

★ **We need to feel significant in our own lives. Then, and only then, can we feel significant in the lives of others**

★ Every time you do something that takes you forwards you feel better; every time you don't you feel worse

★ **Be you. Don't try to be someone else, you won't be very good at it. Be the best version of you and you will do much better than being a poor version of someone else**

★ Just do it. If you do something, then something will happen. If you don't do anything, nothing ever will

★ **Real and sustainable confidence is built on evidence of achievement.**

CHAPTER SEVEN

You're Not As Important As You Think You Are!

....

'Every time I walk down the street people are looking at me, judging me for how I look and what I wear. When I came in here today I felt everyone's eyes on me. I spent ages outside the door, wondering whether to come in or go home.'

....

Those were the words of a participant on a programme I ran for people recovering from mental health problems. I will call her 'Jane'. She was so acutely sensitive about people examining and judging her that she avoided getting into situations where that could happen, severely limiting her ability to meet people, make friends, work or get anything done that involved other people. Just to make it to the workshop had been a battle in itself. Now she was there, she felt that everyone else was staring at her, judging and criticising, laughing, feeling superior. This was someone who continually got in her own way, staying at home, shutting down her possibilities and confirming her negative world view.

You will recognise a number of things that are going on here from previous chapters. Here, Jane has decided the outcome before even making the attempt; she is looking for and easily finding evidence to confirm her prejudices about others; she is giving herself negative self-talk; she is creating a self-fulfilling prophecy; she has low self-esteem and no confidence. These are all behaviours we are now familiar with, but her experience stirs another ingredient into our recipe for stopping ourselves from achieving. This chapter addresses this new ingredient, which we can either call self-consciousness or, if we want to be more judgemental, self-importance.

Self-consciousness is a form of egotism

When Jane described what was happening to her, and as it became increasingly evident that her self-consciousness was impacting on every area of her life and preventing her from living without stress and fear, I said to her: 'You are not as important as you think you are.' She later told me that my words that day had changed her life. Why?

Let's apply some logic to her claim that everyone was staring at her wherever she went and talking about her afterwards. Really? Did she really think she was so important? Would a street full of people walking past and going about their own business be fascinated enough by how she walked and what she was wearing to stop what they were doing, nudge each other and make comments? Their focus would be on themselves, on where they were going and what they were doing, not on her. Their laughter would be nothing to do with her and everything to do with them.

It would be the same with the people on our course. Her fellow participants had come for their own reasons: they were unhappy with aspects of their lives and wanted to make some changes. They may be interested in her as part of their group, but not for the reasons she assumed. Instead they were thinking about their own nerves and their own needs and probably hoping she would be nice, wouldn't think badly of them and could possibly be helpful to them in some way.

....

People in general are not interested in you, they are interested in themselves.

....

We have seen earlier that the most important person in the world to any of us is ourselves, and by extension, our family and significant others. If I'm walking down the street I'm likely to be thinking about myself, my family, my partner, friends, the news, my job or something else of importance to me. I am highly unlikely to be thinking about you. In fact, I probably won't notice you at all. Unless, that is, your own self-consciousness makes you behave in such a way that you draw attention to yourself; maybe by staring at me in a pre-emptive strike, or by looking around you in a furtive way for evidence of people staring at you, or exaggeratedly changing your body posture to appear less conspicuous. Even then, you would have to go some to make a dent in my own preoccupations big enough to draw my attention away from them and onto you. I don't think I'm especially self-obsessed, but on a shopping trip in town I'm thinking about what I'm doing, not what *you're* doing.

This is counter-intuitive, I know, but self-consciousness is, in fact, a form of egotism: you are assuming that you are more important than you are. Jane had convinced herself that everyone else was fascinated by her – they weren't. Once she genuinely accepted that they really had no interest in what she was doing, she was free to do what she wanted.

This form of egotism drives a lot of our self-defeating behaviours and attitudes. It drives the belief that we are uniquely targeted by fate for bad things to happen, or are uniquely prevented by fate from having or doing anything good. No, we're not! Stuff happens. Much of life is random but we can control far more of it than we think. Having a belief that we are being targeted by a malevolent fate or framed by a conspiracy of people who don't like us provides the perfect cover for us to have and do nothing.

'No one likes me' is just as egotistical in its way as 'Everyone loves me'. No, they don't! Some people don't like you and others do, but it's for their own reasons and because of their own interests, ambitions and insecurities. People in general are not interested in you, they are interested in themselves. They will be interested in you only insofar as you have something to offer them or if you can make a contribution to their world as a colleague, a teacher, a rival or a friend.

What other people think

The first thing to say about this is an obvious but largely neglected truth: we don't know what other people think unless we ask them. The second thing is that most of the time what other people think doesn't matter. Now I'm not preaching some form of splendid isolation in which we do exactly what we want and ignore the rights and feelings of others, I'm saying that second-guessing what others think about you or your ideas or ambitions is a waste of time. If their opinion is important to you, ask for it; if it isn't, then don't.

People are more than happy to offer their opinions and to judge others but don't assume that they are doing it for the right reasons or that they have the expertise to make those judgements. I have seen countless examples of someone taking the initiative to do something when no one else has, only for those same people to then criticise that person's efforts. It is so easy to tell someone else what they should do and there is no shortage of people who will do that. The question is whether what they say is either welcome or worth listening to.

· ·

Second-guessing what others think about you or your ideas or ambitions is a waste of time. If their opinion is important to you, ask for it; if it isn't, then don't.

· ·

There are people whose opinion you value and who are worth listening to. As we saw earlier in the section on feedback (page 112), it can be valuable to listen carefully to the views of others, as long as we give ourselves the right to accept or reject them, either in whole or in part. In the end, there is only one opinion that matters more than anyone else's and that, of course, is yours.

....

'My family and friends are the only people I pay mind to. It's none of my business what anyone else thinks. I don't even know them, so why should I care?' Olympic boxer Nicola Adams

....

If you live your life worrying about what other people think then you will be like Jane and allow your life to be defined by others. In her case, her life was governed by what she *imagined* other people were thinking.

As a small child, my favourite book was *The Little Red Hen*. You may remember it – it's the story of a hen who decided she would use the wasted grains of wheat on the farm to make a loaf of bread, and when she asked the other animals to help her, they all refused. They were too lazy to help, they thought it was a stupid idea and didn't believe it could be done. At each stage of the enterprise she asked again and they refused again ('Not I,' said the pig) until the day she baked the bread, at which point they all wanted to help her eat it. I loved the moral of that story: don't listen to the critics who tell you something can't be done, who try to make you feel foolish for trying but won't attempt to do something themselves. You'll find they forget their previous views once you've succeeded!

· ·

If you live your life worrying about what other people think then you will allow your life to be defined by others. More pointlessly still, your life will be governed by what you imagine other people are thinking.

· ·

Nerves and how to overcome them

Conventional wisdom tells us that we need to have a certain amount of nerves in order to perform well, otherwise we get complacent and our performance dips. Nerves, people will tell us, give us that little 'edge' and keep us on our toes. I don't disagree with that, but I still think we are sensible if we remove excess or unnecessary nerves through research, training and clarifying what we want to achieve and why.

After I had given a presentation to a lecture theatre full of people someone asked me if I ever got nervous. My honest answer was no – unless I hadn't prepared properly. If I'm prepared then I know I can deal with whatever comes up, but if not, the risk of failure or disaster is much bigger for all sorts of reasons that by this chapter we are already familiar with.

Being prepared enables me to focus on the here and now rather than the past or future. This is essential to getting the best out of myself and the situation. If I allow the **past** to get into my head while I'm working, I allow myself to think unproductive thoughts that take my focus away from what I'm doing now. For example, in the recent past I may have made some mistakes, including not preparing properly, for which I'm inclined to beat myself up a bit and ask myself damning questions. Why didn't I spend time preparing? Why didn't I research who was going to be in the audience? Why didn't I include that great idea I had last week? Why don't I ever prepare properly? Why am I such an idiot?

If I think too much about the **future**, I may worry about the *consequences* of what I'm doing instead of focusing on doing it well *in the moment*. I let a different set of random and pointless questions into my head. What if they don't like what I'm doing? What if I've misinterpreted the brief? What if I look or sound stupid? What if I'm not as good as I think I am?

. . . .

*All you can control is the **here and now**. If you focus on what you are doing now and what you can control, you will do it much better than if you focus on things you can't control; things like the past or the future.*

. . . .

All you can control is the **here and now**. If you focus on what you are doing now and what you can control, you will do it much better than if you focus on things you can't control; things like the past or the future.

I run 'train the trainer' courses for people who want to prepare for delivering training sessions. When I tell them that as part of the course they will be delivering a short session to the rest of the group, most people naturally feel a little uneasy and will worry about how they might do. A certain amount of nerves may help their performance by ensuring they take it seriously and put in the right amount of effort. Others, however, feel something closer to panic at the thought of presenting to the group: panic is not useful.

I work through these feelings with them by encouraging them to stop thinking about themselves and start thinking instead about their audience. If you are running a training session then you are responsible for making it as good as you can, but that doesn't mean the session is about *you*, it's about the *group*. Using the principle of not being as important as we think we are, if we can shift our focus from us to them, then we will remove our unproductive obsession with ourselves. I know because I've been through the same journey myself.

When I deliver a talk or training session people only care about me to the extent that what I do affects them. They've come to learn, or be entertained, or work with the others in the group, they haven't come to think about me. It's remarkable how much that shift in focus removes unnecessary nerves and enables me to be there in the present, engage with the topic and the people and be of much more value to them.

Nerves are natural and they serve a purpose, but there's no point in having them unnecessarily. They can help you perform but in themselves they are overrated, so avoid nerves caused by your own insecurities or lack of preparation. The nerves you then feel are much more likely to be brought on by your energy and commitment to high standards rather than your ego; those nerves you can use to help you focus and they can be transformed into ideas and activity.

In the 'zone'

If you remove all the 'rubbish' you have allowed to accumulate in your brain you will gain clarity. This is a precious commodity as most of us simply don't allow the space in our heads to think clearly or 'sift' through the mountain of debris that obscures our vision and blocks our path.

Have you had the experience of deciding to do something with your day and getting to the end of it and finding that despite being 'busy' all day you've got nowhere near to doing what you planned? I think we all have days like this, and far too many of them! Why does this happen?

Without clarity you have no focus, so your mind shoots off in all sorts of directions and you can't settle to anything. You start one thing and then abandon it for something else, or you have a third cup of coffee instead (more of that in the next chapter), or you run up against a problem and decide to start something else instead. Each false start and each abandonment only reinforces your perception of yourself as not being capable of achieving what you set out to achieve, and from there, it's a short step to all the bad habits of negative thinking that we've talked about so far.

This is a cycle of behaviour, and the problem with cycles of behaviour is that each time you go around the same loop, you entrench it still further. Criticism from a boss or a loved one seems justified and your frustration increases, with the world and yourself and whatever it is you're trying to do. This lets the rubbish pile up and confirms all your negative self-talk. 'I'm *never* going to get anywhere with this,' you say. 'What's the point? Why does this always happen to me? Who am I trying to kid?' All the absolute statements (*always, never*) and all the rhetorical questions take the place of logic, planning and, crucially, action.

The world of sport is a great metaphor for life and provides some concepts we can make good use of in our quest to improve our performance. Sportspeople have to remove exactly this kind of muddled thinking in order to enter important competitions in the peak of physical and mental condition. Few of us will be able to call on the mental discipline of a Nicola Adams (see also page 124), but few of us need to; all we need to do is improve our discipline enough to perform better than we are and keep on improving it.

We have already looked at the concept of purposeful practice as a means of preparing ourselves for success (see also page 38). A second concept that applies to all of us is what appears to be a slightly more mysterious one, which becomes far less mysterious and much more logical with a little analysis. This is the concept of being 'in the zone'.

When an athlete or indeed a performer of any kind reaches a state of effortless mastery of their trade they are described as being 'in the zone'. Those who have experienced this phenomenon talk of time appearing to slow down so they have all the time in the world to see an opportunity, react to it and do exactly what they pictured themselves doing. They may be surrounded by others racing to get to the ball or the finishing line first but they have no impact on the athlete's ability to deliver. How and why does this happen? And how can we access this state?

The 'zone' is, in fact, easy to explain. The athlete has achieved a state of preparation in which his or her mind and body is perfectly tuned in to their environment. They have honed their skills to the point where they can perform automatically and can recognise and understand all the information coming at them from all directions. This what Malcolm Gladwell, in his book *Outliers*, refers to as 'genius' and is the result of absolute focus over many years. In *Blink*, he describes a fireman ordering his team to leave a burning building seconds before it explodes, without consciously knowing why – his subconscious did the job for him, based on his in-depth knowledge of how fires behave.

Have you ever had the experience of leaving a situation you were unhappy with – an argument perhaps, or the scene of a humiliation – and delivering the perfect speech in your head, utterly destroying all the points raised by your adversary? You probably find yourself wishing you could have delivered that speech at the time, and lamenting you don't have the ability to do it. However, the fact that you did deliver that speech, if only in your head, shows that you do, in fact, possess that ability – you just haven't honed the skills to be able to do it when you need to.

I used to play a lot of football and I was quite good at it, but not great. I wasn't blessed with great confidence and at my worst would miss open goals because I was too busy worrying about missing them. I'm not alone, as the ex-footballer Tony Cascarino illustrates in his autobiography, *Full Time*, when describing in excruciating detail missing an open goal for Celtic in an Old Firm derby against Rangers in front of 80,000 fans. Cascarino says he actively talked himself into missing when it would have been easier to score. Instead he allowed the enormity of the situation to enter his head, leading him to think about the implications of messing up a gilt-edged opportunity to be a hero, and this took away his ability to do what should have been the automatic result of years of honing his skills.

....

If you remove all the 'rubbish' you have allowed to accumulate in your brain you will gain clarity. This is a precious commodity as most of us simply don't allow the space in our heads to think clearly or 'sift' through the mountain of debris that obscures our vision and blocks our path.

....

One week from my footballing 'career' (spent in Sunday League and works teams) stands out in my mind, when I was playing virtually all the time. I scored a hat-trick on Sunday for one team, five in midweek for another and then one on Saturday for a third. An incredible nine goals in seven days and three matches! I can still see every detail of a superb goal I scored in the second game (no room for false modesty in this book!), and I see it as I did at the time, in slow motion, with a complete awareness of where the goalkeeper was, and where the defender was, who was trying to close me down: the 'zone' is real.

When we get very good at our jobs, whether playing an instrument, running, filing, teaching, operating machinery, driving, talking or writing, we can enter our version of the zone, where we do things automatically. Driving home on a familiar route we can find ourselves several miles further on than we thought, without remembering doing it. This is because we no longer need to consciously think about what we are doing. Not great for driving perhaps, but it shows what we are capable of if we rid ourselves of the rubbish.

Judging yourself and being judged

Let's go back to Jane for a moment. She actively prevented herself from creating opportunities and reacting positively to them because she allowed a faulty assumption to get in her way: she judged herself and judged others on the basis of a fiction of her own making. Jane is not alone in making this kind of mistake. People decide what they are capable of and what they are not without any recourse to evidence. They assign motives to others that are not there and prejudge the outcomes of their actions before they have taken them.

But Jane was able to reflect on her automatic behaviour and change it. She moved beyond her destructive self-consciousness and started seeing a world beyond herself. Now she no longer assumes people are interested in her because she knows that they are interested in themselves first and foremost, and she knows that is a good thing. A wonderful side-effect of this new perspective on life is that because no one is judging her, she no longer needs to judge herself.

Jane is now working in a job she loves and feels that she is making a worthwhile contribution; she has new friends and renewed confidence and neither expects people to judge her nor cares if they do. She has cleared away her rubbish and her life is all the better for it. Yours can be too.

You're Not As Important As You Think You Are!
Takeaways from Chapter Seven

★ Second-guessing what others think about you or your ideas or ambitions is a waste of time. If their opinion is important to you, ask for it; if it isn't, then don't!

★ **People in general are not interested in you, they are interested in themselves**

★ If you live your life worrying about what other people think you will allow your life to be defined by others. More pointlessly still, your life will be governed by what you *imagine* other people are thinking

★ **All you can control is the** here and now**. If you focus on what you are doing now and what you can control you will do it much better than if you focus on things you can't control; things like the past or the future**

★ If you remove all the 'rubbish' you have allowed to accumulate in your brain then you will gain clarity. This is a precious commodity as most of us simply don't allow the space in our heads to think clearly or 'sift' through the mountain of debris that obscures our vision and blocks our path.

CHAPTER EIGHT

Displacement, Avoidance and Delay (Why We Do It and Where It Leads Us)

Mind the Gap

We've covered some big issues in this book, and they are all important to your aim of getting out of your own way. I'm now going to ask you to switch your focus to a lot of little things instead. Most of them are not important and not worth your time or attention but they are going to take up most of this chapter. Why? Because they take up most of your time.

Anyone who has travelled on the London Underground will be familiar with the recorded voice that warns us to 'Mind the gap'. It's very good advice, but the gap I'm concerned with is not the gap between the edge of the train and the platform. If I think back over past failures and disappointments I can trace a lot of them back to the simple but all-important gap between thinking and doing. Had I gone ahead and done what I knew I needed to do, I know that in virtually every case I would have made progress. If I had actually done something instead of finding reasons not to, I would have achieved so much more. I know that because of the opportunities I missed and the ones I took: I achieved little when I held back and a lot when I went for it. I stress again that here I'm not talking about the bigger concepts we've tackled so far but our daily habits instead. A few small examples can serve to make the larger point:

Forgetfulness. I've always regarded my poor memory as the reason I forget to do things. Now I'm convinced that it's a symptom, not a cause. I don't think I forget things at all. What I do is remember them at various times during the day but neglect to take action. One evening, I was due to meet a friend and had some things I was supposed to bring with me. On arrival I found I had forgotten them – one item was left on the arm of a chair, another in my office and a third was in a reminder on my phone. I had remembered them all, but had either partially dealt with them or not dealt with them at all. Instead I had created a gap between thinking and doing, and every single one of those tasks fell through that gap. That's not forgetfulness, it's not taking responsibility for following something through.

Absent-mindedness. Where was I? Ah, yes! If you are absent, it simply means you are not present. It's a choice – I chose not to pick up those items and put them in my car ready for the journey, so when I drove away, they weren't there. I might forget where I left my glasses or what I went upstairs for, or even what I was going to do with my life. Lots of little things add up to one big thing. There is no excuse for not being present in your own life.

Organisation. I didn't bother to make a list or organise myself in preparation for going out. That isn't laziness but it *is* lack of organisation. A few seconds of thinking and planning would have prevented me from letting people down. There have been many occasions where I've let *myself* down for the same reason, or at least made things much harder for myself and others than they needed to be.

In order to make progress we need to do things to help the process along. If we don't do those things, the process stalls. Everything in life is a process – it all depends on something else to make it happen. Processes need to be efficient and effective, and few would argue that a business needs to be well-run or a factory clean and well-organised, but when it comes to producing great results for ourselves, we seem to think we can make it up as we go along.

The truth is if we want to get things done then we need to accept that our ambitions can only be achieved with a clear vision and some discipline. We need to set goals, break them down into manageable targets, prepare ourselves, take action and continuously improve our processes if we want to give ourselves the best chance of success.

If you read the autobiography of any successful individual there is one quality that stands out above all else: discipline. There are a lot of talented people in the world who don't achieve because they don't make the effort. I'm not talking about an occasional effort followed by a longer period of retreat but a sustained effort: this means keeping going until you have actually completed something. Successful people may have less natural talent but they more than make up for it with commitment, discipline and hard work. Doesn't sound much fun, does it? I promise you it's much more fun than not doing it at all.

This chapter is a practical and honest exploration of all the little things we do and don't do that together make a massive difference to our ability to live a productive and purposeful life, whatever your purpose is.

Busy doing nothing

Time: we don't know how much time we will have and yet we routinely forget how precious it is. In 'A Sunday Afternoon At Home', another BBC Radio 4 *Hancock's Half Hour*, our hero spends the day complaining about how bored he is and saying how much he hates Sundays. Eventually Sid James's character turns on him: 'There's one a week and there always has been and there always will be, so shut up and get on with it!' Hancock responds by saying next week he might take one of his pills on Saturday night and wake up on Monday morning when it's over.

Conceptually, we know how precious time is and how quickly it passes, but practically, that knowledge makes little difference to how we behave. We routinely fritter time away doing anything but the things that will help us to achieve what we want to achieve, or be where we want to be. Think of the hours spent watching TV, often not really watching it at all but vaguely following the images and words as they slip by, or flicking through the channels trying to find something that will divert us. Divert us from what? From our inspiration? Our goals? Our families? Our lives?

Millions spend their time compulsively checking their devices for mail or social media updates. Many of us doze gently in our armchairs late into the night instead of going to bed and sleeping properly, and then wake the next morning unrested and out of sorts with the world. All the while there are family members we could be talking to, hobbies we could be enjoying and skills we could be learning and perfecting. Yet when we think about what we really want to be doing we tell ourselves that we don't have time. It's the most common excuse people give for not starting something, or giving it up before they've succeeded. The passing of time is not a choice, but what we do with our time is up to us. You make things happen by doing stuff, and the only place we can do stuff is the time available to do it in: as the poet Philip Larkin asked, *'Where can we live but days?*

So, why is it so difficult to focus on what we want and to do it? Why is it so much more attractive to do something else, something meaningless or unproductive; in fact, *anything* that isn't what we really want or need to do? In the words of the old nonsense song, for great chunks of time we're 'busy doing nothing, working the whole day through, trying to find lots of things not to do'.

....

The passing of time is not a choice, but what we do with our time is up to us.

....

Let's identify some of the ways we busy ourselves doing nothing, understand why we do them, the implications of our behaviour and how we can abandon those behaviours instead of abandoning our dreams.

Procrastination

This one word covers a multitude of sins, causes a whole raft of problems and has many causes. Someone should write a book about it! Everything we have explored up to this point contributes to procrastination, which is a catch-all word for describing the act of putting things off, delaying action and avoiding responsibility. If you have a tendency to leave things until the last minute or beyond, to agonise over making decisions or to avoid commitment, then you are a procrastinator. If you're a serial procrastinator then you risk never getting anything done, and even when you do, it won't be as good as it should be, or as thorough, or as effective or enjoyable either.

Why do we procrastinate? It will be different for all of us, according to our background, our issues and our psyche, but that's no reason not to address it as a topic and deal with it. Thinking that something is too complicated or personal to deal with is, after all, a form of procrastination in itself. In my work I find variants on a common phrase from individuals in all sorts of situations: 'It's different for us', 'It's more complicated for me', 'It's all right for you to say that, but . . .' Because of the particular circumstances we are in we hide behind reasons for not getting started on the things we most want to achieve: it's because of Mum, my job, my family, working overtime, money, being young/old, my industry, my education, my gender, my character. In our uniqueness we are all the same.

....

'Procrastination is the thief of time,' says the old adage. If you allow your time to be stolen then you allow your life to be stolen with it.

....

We procrastinate for all sorts of reasons. Here are a few of them: fear of failure, fear of success, fear of not doing something well enough, fear of being judged; feelings of guilt, inadequacy or embarrassment; trying to predict the future fifteen steps ahead instead of dealing with what's right in front of us, so that we end up planning how to avoid the negative consequences of something that will not even happen. What a tiring list! All that fear, all those negative feelings, all that worry . . . What a waste of energy! Imagine if we could expend as much energy on doing stuff as we routinely spend on not doing it.

Procrastination is illogical and counterproductive. In delaying doing something we either want or need to do we are trying to avoid the negative consequences that might arise from doing it. What we are actually avoiding are imaginary consequences, because they haven't happened yet, but we have decided they *might* happen. In a pre-emptive strike we therefore avoid doing something that may bring about those results. It's a cowardly response to an imagined future and is a form of self-talk. We are not sitting somewhere thinking about all the wonderful things that we can make happen by taking action, instead we are worrying about all the dreadful things that could happen if we do. In other words, we are avoiding the blame for things that will never happen. Really, what the hell are we doing to ourselves?

So let's make an agreement here before we move on to address some more aspects of displacement, avoidance and delay. Let's accept the logic that it is healthier and more useful for us to deal with what is actually happening than what we *think* might happen at some point in the future. This is the only way to kick procrastination into touch. Let's agree something else as well: it starts now.

....

Let's accept the logic that it is healthier and more useful for us to deal with what is actually happening than what we think might happen at some point in the future. This is the only way to kick procrastination into touch.

....

Displacement activities

Much of our time is spent, or frittered away, doing things that don't have a purpose. They are not taking us towards our goal and there is nothing inherently valuable in doing them. The main 'virtue' for us of displacement activities is that while we are doing them we are not doing something else.

When we're engaged in pointless activity we don't need to face up to anything other than filling our time. Some displacement activities enable us to pretend that we were doing something productive, such as putting things in piles on our desks, making lists or even surfing the Net. Others are just pointless, however we try to dress them up: making a tenth cup of coffee that we don't even want, creating chains out of paperclips or playing cards on our phones.

Displacement activities are defined by *The Oxford Advanced Learning Dictionary* as '*things that you do in order to avoid doing what you are supposed to be doing*'. This is as good a description as any. We know we have a challenge to meet or a task to complete and we don't want to do it, so we are caught between two impulses: we want to resolve the situation by doing whatever it is or by not doing it, so we are conflicted by two contrasting drives.

We need to do *something* in order to satisfy the tension created by the choice in front of us, so we do *something else*. The key requirement is that what we are doing has nothing at all to do with the actual task or decision we are supposed to be dealing with, it's an efficient method of avoiding real work or real responsibility.

....

Displacement activities are experienced as pleasurable, so we seek them out instead of the pain of doing something difficult, but it's the difficult thing that gives us the long-term results we are really seeking.

....

Next time you find yourself laying out all your odd socks in a row and trying to pair them up (an eminently sensible thing to do, of course), ask yourself if you're doing it because you need to pair up your socks *right now* or because you need to do something difficult and important. If so, do the important stuff now and sort your socks into pairs with a cup of coffee and your favourite album playing, and reflect on how much better you feel now you've accomplished something.

My biggest and longest contract was the direct result of me phoning someone I only knew a little. It took a bit of effort to make the call and some discomfort at the thought of doing so, but we met up for a coffee (just the one, and it was a useful one!) six years ago and I have been working with him ever since. The more you do, the more there is to do, but that's a good thing. Keep doing the important things and you won't feel the need to fill your time with distraction and delay.

....

The more you do, the more there is to do, but that's a good thing. Keep doing the important things and you won't feel the need to fill your time with distraction and delay.

....

Avoiding unpleasant tasks

We are programmed to seek pleasure and avoid pain, which makes sense. Who in their right mind would actively prefer to experience pain than pleasure (answers on a postcard please)? The difficulty is that sometimes we attach these labels to the wrong things – for example, smoking is labelled for some people as pleasure when the reality is that it is damaging their health and fitness so logically should be filed under pain. A committed smoker will therefore ignore the advice of health professionals, friends and family and continue to associate smoking with pleasure and therefore resist all attempts to make them give it up.

We all file activities under pain and pleasure and behave accordingly. What the smoker fails to do is to recognise the long-term benefits of overcoming these classifications, so smoking is always pleasure and giving up is always pain. They want to continue doing something they enjoy and will come up with all sorts of reasons in support of their position, invoking the right to make their own decisions, and casting overbearing 'experts' and a nanny state as straw men to fight against. Citing free will as an argument in favour of addiction shows the extent to which logic deserts us once we've made up our minds to resist.

The aim is to switch the headings, so that smoking equals pain and all the benefits of good health equal pleasure. This is difficult to do, as we have invested so much in keeping the status quo that we are programmed to deflect or destroy every weapon deployed against our investment. Success depends on our ability to recognise that there is a goal that's worth making a sacrifice for, and that the previously favoured option (smoking) is preventing us from achieving that goal. For the smoker it might be their wish to be alive long enough to see their grandchildren grow up and be fit enough to play with them. What is it for you that will turn your perceptions around?

Displacement activities are experienced as pleasurable, so we seek them out instead of the pain of doing something difficult, but it's the difficult thing that gives us the long-term results we are really seeking.

....

We spend a lot of our time doing things we shouldn't be doing, often as a way of avoiding doing the things we should be doing. Try doing the important things instead.

....

In his useful book on time management and productivity, *Eat That Frog!*, Brian Tracy describes these unpleasant tasks as frogs that need to be eaten. Eating a frog is not a nice or easy thing to do so we put it off until later. Once it is 'later' there are a whole set of different reasons for us not to eat it, so we keep putting it off until later still. These 'frogs' are invariably the most important things on our agenda at any one time, and therefore the task that needs to be done first, but we leave them until last, preferring to fill our time with less onerous activities.

Unless we eat our frogs sooner rather than later we will be using up all our time with less important things, leaving the most important things undone. Tasks become frogs because they are important to us and impact on our success, but if we attach too much importance to them they can become intimidating. We then avoid them because our brain senses discomfort and associates them with pain, which in turn means we avoid them. It's a circular argument and a recipe for being busy without doing anything productive.

If we do the difficult but important thing first then we will make much quicker progress towards where we want to be; we will also gain satisfaction from doing it, can learn from the experience and reflect afterwards on our courage and discipline. In doing so we will be on the way towards taking control of our thoughts, our actions and our future.

Perfectionism

The perfectionist is his or her own harshest critic. Whatever they do is never quite enough and they are never truly satisfied. So, is perfectionism a good or a bad thing? The answer is yes.

The drive to continuously improve is good, driving you on to perform even better and achieve even more. Indeed the dedication of a perfectionist can produce amazing results as the desire for perfection gives the focus and discipline that pushes you forwards and keeps you going when things don't go your way. It can help you to master difficult skills and gain deep knowledge of your subject when others take shortcuts and skim over the surface. But perfectionism can also stop you in your tracks and ensure you never get off the starting block. If nothing is ever good enough, this can be a reason to decide not to bother trying. Many people with perfectionist tendencies will take one look at the person they want to emulate or the goal they wish to achieve and decide that they will never match up to it, no matter how hard they try. If they can't do it perfectly, why do it at all?

If you use an ideal of perfection as a stick to beat yourself up with then it will be counterproductive. But if you use it as a yardstick to measure your progress against then noticing your improvements can be motivating. Being 'perfect' can mean that you don't do anything until you can be confident that you will do it perfectly. Can we guarantee this? No, we can't. Therefore, if your overriding aim is to be perfect, it follows that a lot of the time you won't do anything meaningful at all. As we have already seen, if you don't do anything you can't make anything else happen, so your drive for perfectionism can easily become a drive towards standstill.

You are not perfect – hopefully, you never will be. Your task, should you choose to accept it (and you wouldn't have got this far through the book if you didn't want to), is to work on yourself and your dreams in a spirit of continuous growth and development. The more disciplined you are, the better your results will be, but this is not a punishment course and every step is there to be enjoyed – otherwise, what's the point of it all? I think of our task as to be the best we can be: not necessarily *the* best, but the best that *we* can be. That's a pretty good aim, and achieving it will come as close to that elusive goal of perfection as you need to be.

Doing the wrong things

We live in a state in which we feel the pressure to 'do' something all the time. It's a state of constant activity, one of the results of which is that we get tired. We are tired because of the constant rush of activity and also because we are aware of all the things we should be doing that we are not doing. One of the things this leads to is 'burnout' – a condition most commonly associated with top executives and sometimes worn by them as a badge of honour. I think there's a case for inventing a new syndrome of our own, something along the lines of 'switch-off' or 'never set alight' syndrome, in which we are so worn out from doing all the wrong things that we have nothing left when it comes to doing the things we should be doing.

Throughout this book I have advised that we can only get things done by doing things, so I know that here I am also reinforcing this message of taking action. I stand by that, as nothing gets done if you don't do anything, but it is important that we do the right things. David Allen's book, *Getting Things Done*, contains a technique he calls the 'What's the next action?' decision. His argument is that we are so conditioned to responding to what's in front of us that we spend our time shuffling things around, trying to remember them and failing to prioritise effectively enough to deal with them. We typically carry around in our heads a whole load of priorities and things that need to get done. They clamour for our attention and we think about them dozens of times a day without actually dealing with them – just as I 'forgot' to do several things before meeting my friend earlier in this chapter.

We spend a lot of our time doing things we shouldn't be doing, often as a way of avoiding doing the things we should be doing. Allen's 'What's the next action?' technique requires us to decide for any given task what the next thing is that we need to do to resolve it or take it forward to the next step – and then do it. For example, if the next thing to do is to put something in the car so I won't drive off without it, that's what I do. If you need to talk to someone, you go and talk to them. He describes it as 'creating the option of doing'. If you need to do something you promised yourself yesterday that you would do today, do it. Then it's done.

So, mind the gap between thinking and doing, or you will miss the train.

Displacement, Avoidance and Delay
(Why We Do It and Where It Leads Us):
Takeaways from Chapter Eight

★ The passing of time is not a choice, but what we do with our time is up to us

★ *'Procrastination is the thief of time,'* says the old adage. If you allow your time to be stolen then you allow your *life* to be stolen with it

★ Let's accept the logic that it is healthier and more useful for us to deal with what is actually happening than what we think might happen at some point in the future. This is the only way to kick procrastination into touch

★ **The more you do, the more there is to do, but that's a good thing. Keep doing the important things and you won't feel the need to fill your time with distractions and delays**

★ Displacement activities are experienced as pleasurable, so we seek them out instead of the pain of doing something difficult, but it's the difficult thing that gives us the long-term results we are really seeking

★ **We spend a lot of our time doing things we shouldn't be doing, often as a way to avoid doing the things we should be doing. Try doing the important things instead!**

CHAPTER NINE

Dreams, Goals and Targets: What's the Difference – And Does It Matter Anyway?

'If one advances confidently in the direction of his dreams, and endeavors to live the life which he has imagined, he will meet with a success unexpected in common hours.' Henry David Thoreau

When is a goal not a goal?

There is a lot of advice out there about setting and achieving goals or targets and having dreams, missions and visions. A lot of it is contradictory and some of it is almost intimidating in the evangelical fervour with which it is presented. We are told to have BHAGs (Big Hairy Audacious Goals) but also to be realistic so we don't set ourselves up to fail; to break down bigger goals into smaller steps and to make big leaps across the chasm; that the journey starts with the first step and that we should start with the end in mind; to create SMART goals (Specific, Measurable, Achievable, Relevant and Timed); to set a specific goal for every area of your life (such as fitness and health, financial, career, family); to continually review our goals to ensure they are still relevant and to set milestones and monitor progress against them. We're also told (in research articles from *Psychology Today* and others) that setting goals doesn't work at all but instead creates a sense of failure in those who don't achieve them and can even distort behaviour.

Beneath all the real and pseudo-science a goal is simply a way of *defining* what you want to achieve and *planning* the *actions* you will need to take in order to achieve it. A goal 'statement' on its own, such as 'I want to be wealthy', is not a goal at all. It's a dream, just another way of saying you wish your life was different and better than it is right now. That sort of dreaming, while harmless in itself, gets you nowhere. If, however, you feel disappointed, frustrated, victimised, hopeless or any of a host of bad emotions about yourself or the world in general because you are not wealthy, then we can say that your dream is doing you harm.

· ·

The very fact of creating goals for yourself increases your chances of success compared to those who don't set them at all.

· ·

Before you can begin to justify any of those feelings of victimhood it is worth reflecting on what you personally can do to change your situation – this is what a goal is for. A goal will translate your dream of wealth into something quantifiable that you can start to work towards. Some people want to be famous, others prefer to just be popular; some want to be admired, others just want to be respected; some wish to influence others while some just want to be listened to every now and again. In this chapter we will work to build an effective goal or two for you that will include the elements you need to translate the goal into reality. I won't make any promises that you will go on to achieve it, but I *can* show you the building blocks and you can then take your goal with you into the rest of your life and see what happens. It's better than complaining, isn't it?

Do goals 'distort' behaviour?

Yes, they do, and that's entirely the point. If they didn't distort behaviour then they wouldn't be worth setting. Incidentally, the word 'distort' has negative connotations and I can see where the opponents of goals are coming from, so let's replace that word with something more positive such as 'improve', or something neutral, such as 'influence' or 'change'. Bad goals distort, good goals influence and great goals improve. All we need to do is to make sure that the goals we set are, in fact, the ones we want to set – goals that mean something to us, that speak to our core values and wishes; goals that belong to us and no one else.

One thing is undeniable: the very fact of creating goals for yourself increases your chances of success compared to those who don't set them at all. Having a goal creates a sense of direction so you know where you're heading; it gives you a purpose, a reason for putting in that little bit of extra effort. Anyone who has ever achieved anything has had the key elements of an effective goal in their lives to guide them in whatever they need to do and where they need to be. These elements are focus, passion, belief and commitment.

Focus. Humans are goal-seeking creatures. In other words, we are much more effective when we have something to work towards. Here, I am emphatically not suggesting that we can only be happy if chained to the yoke of personal improvement to the exclusion of happiness now: if you are content with where you are, you don't need to do anything different. Just enjoy it and appreciate the people who share it with you. If you are not happy with one or more aspects of your life, however, then feeling sorry for yourself is not a permanent solution, and having a goal to aim for will be enormously helpful to you.

. . . .

If you are content with where you are, you don't need to do anything different. Just enjoy it and appreciate the people who share it with you.

. . . .

Think about some of your happiest times and you will probably remember when life was simple and everything was clear. Depending on your personal history this may be a time when you had nothing to do but focus on the here and now, in the way a contented child can with endless time and resources in front of them. It may be working closely with others in a team (work, sports, a band, a family) and working to achieve something incredible. Or it might be working on your own to achieve something that really means a lot to you.

I count as one of my happiest times the last few weeks of my student life when everything was focused on three weeks of finals exams and nothing else mattered. The evening beer tasted so much better after a day's revision than after a day of idleness, and the knowledge on waking of what I had to do was motivating in its clarity and purpose. Not everyone's cup of tea, I'm sure, but I loved the simplicity and focus of it, and the hard work.

What all of these happy experiences share is the satisfaction of knowing what you need to do. When your life has focus everything is so much clearer than when you live without a purpose. If you have no focus, no goal, nothing to work towards, then how can you decide what is important and what isn't? With a meaningful goal you can make decisions easily because you know the basis on which you are deciding: will it take me towards my goal or away from it? Focus your attention and you focus your time, your energy and your attention on the right things – and you will feel so much better for doing it.

Passion. There is no point in setting a goal you don't care enough about. Any goal we set must include within it the reason for doing it: we won't work to achieve something we don't feel invested in; we won't take ownership of the work involved or responsibility for making sure it gets done to the best of our ability. We will only achieve a goal if we give our best in terms of effort, attitude and attention to detail and we simply won't bother if we don't care whether we achieve it or not. A lot of people feel like this about their jobs, which is a pity as they spend so much of their lives doing them.

. . . .

Whatever your goal, you need to want it with passion; there has to be pleasure in it, enjoyment, fun, triumph, victory over yourself, your fears, perceived adversity, whatever it is that means something to you. Nothing beats setting yourself a challenging goal, even one that you or others assumed was impossible, and achieving it.

. . . .

You don't need to be passionate about your job. It's great if you can be, and it's a good idea to work with your manager and other colleagues to put a bit of passion into your work to improve your performance. In my first book, *Management Starts With You*, I describe managing a team that went from forty-third in the country to first by following these steps and it was a great experience for everyone involved. One colleague described it as 'the happiest I've ever been at work'.

You do need to be passionate about something, however, if you genuinely want to feel the deep sense of satisfaction that comes with achievement.

· ·

A colleague of mine worked in an office job for years without feeling even remotely passionate about what he was doing. He came into work at nine, left at five, and did what he had to do. He did this for decades. His passion was playing saxophone in clubs with his jazz trio. He worked as a session musician and met his musical heroes. Work was a means to an end, enabling him to support his family and be a musician. He didn't resent his unfulfilling job, he followed his passion. There's an example of work–life balance!

· ·

Whatever your goal, you need to want it with passion; there has to be pleasure in it, enjoyment, fun, triumph, victory over yourself, your fears, perceived adversity, whatever it is that means something to you. *Nothing* beats setting yourself a challenging goal, even one that you or others assumed was impossible, and achieving it.

Belief. If you don't believe you can do something, you won't do it. Anyone who has asked a teenager to do something like tidy their room or get up on time and had the response 'I'll try' knows they may as well do it themselves! Belief in your ability is essential, but if you don't start out with that belief it doesn't mean you won't succeed. Belief is built through evidence of achievement, so just as we saw with self-esteem in Chapter Six, the best way to build the confidence you need to succeed is to start succeeding.

....

If you don't believe you can do something, you won't do it.

....

There are a lot of individual actions to take on the way to achieving anything worthwhile and as the ancient Chinese philosopher Lao Tzui said, 'a journey of a thousand miles begins with the first step'. Simply taking that first step is enough to reinforce your belief that you can make the whole journey. The first time I spoke in front of a room full of colleagues my throat dried up and the pen shook in my hand as I wrote on the flipchart. Now I make my living delivering courses to groups of all sizes and people from all walks of life. Having done something that you found difficult you can look back on it, feel proud of having made the attempt and use what you've learnt about yourself and the task to improve on the next one.

Belief can also come from your passion. If it is really so important to you to do something, you can always find a way to do it. Business magnate Richard Branson's advice to entrepreneurs is good, no less so for being a little selfish and irresponsible. He says, 'If someone asks you to do something you don't know how to do, say yes. Then learn how to do it.' His point is that you shouldn't be put off by your *current* lack of knowledge or experience. As with most entrepreneurial types, what is important to their success is having the confidence to do something even when they know they are not quite ready. Perfectionists, take note – you can get ready in time to do it!

Some cultures, including the British culture, are uncomfortable with confidence. If someone is 'too sure of themselves' we see them as arrogant or 'above themselves' and part of us secretly looks forward to seeing them 'brought down a peg or two'. I experience this sometimes when reading otherwise excellent American self-help books, when I find myself thinking, *this guy is just a little bit too pleased with himself*! Instinctively, I prefer my guides not to be too self-aggrandising. It's very British of me, and quite unfair. If someone has succeeded in what they do and has a great reputation, why shouldn't he or she be proud of it and have sky-high self-èsteem if s/he wants to?

We see this aspect of our psyche reflected in parts of the media, which are more than happy to support someone on their way up, but then start knocking them once they've arrived. As the actor Charlton Heston once said of the press: 'They build you up to knock you down.' I think we do that to ourselves as well, through unhelpful beliefs based perhaps on messages from others, experience of past failures and embarrassments or from our cultural norms.

Don't worry about appearing overconfident, as long as that doesn't make you complacent. Complacency is a different thing altogether and is to be avoided at all costs as it makes you intellectually flabby and mentally lazy. You will need the confidence to try, the humility to know you won't always succeed and the determination to learn from the experience and try again. You and I are unlikely to suffer overconfidence or any form of vainglory, and are more likely to be intimidated by someone who demonstrates these things, but if we do find ourselves getting 'above our station' then great! And if I've helped you in my small way, my work is done.

Commitment. Singer-songwriter Bruce Springsteen describes in his autobiography the night he played at the annual Rock & Roll Hall of Fame. He found himself onstage between Mick Jagger and George Harrison, a Stone and a Beatle, singing into the same microphone. Those were the heroes who had inspired him to pick up a guitar in the first place and now he was sharing a stage with them. He describes his journey to that point, from thinking music looked fun, buying a guitar, joining a local band, making a demo tape, getting a record deal, selling some records, touring, having a hit, earning a living and finally achieving fame and fortune. At each stage, many young men fell away, leaving him as *the one* who ended up where he did. 'My parents were right,' he says, 'My chances were one in a million. But still . . . here I was. I knew my talents and I worked hard, but these were the gods and I was one hard working guitar man.' His point was that there were thousands of young men who wanted what he did, but they didn't get it. But he did. There was luck and circumstance and talent in the mix as well, but it was his hard work and undying commitment that singled him out for the main prize.

Springsteen wouldn't have been able to put in that commitment if he didn't love music. He didn't set a formal SMART goal or write it down on a piece of paper but he knew in his heart what he was going to do and he did everything that was necessary to achieve it: he had a goal, he had passion, he believed he would do it, and that all gave him the commitment to follow it through. A similar mix can be found in the stories of anyone who has set out their stall to achieve something big, something that is an expression of who they really are and who they would like to be.

Focus, passion and belief are essentials, but commitment is where the magic happens. Once you commit to doing something, really commit to it, you are on your way. And if you keep committing, you become unstoppable.

When we start on a course of action we are not where we want to be and we want to be somewhere else instead. That doesn't mean dreaming about being there (pleasant as that can be), wishing we were already there (tempting as that is) or blaming others because we aren't there (comforting as that may be in the short-term). Those are all recipes for staying exactly where we are.

Commitment is different from thinking about doing something, planning to do it or saying you will do it: commitment means *deciding* to do it. Once you have committed, you set in train all the positive goal-seeking and problem-solving tools at your brain's disposal and these, as we saw in Chapter Two (page 25), are formidable. Because our brains dislike tension, we want to resolve that tension in the quickest and most effective way possible. Once we have committed, this is a firm 'instruction' to our subconscious to go and get the result we need, as this is now the only way for it to fulfil that instruction and resolve the tension.

....

Focus, passion and belief are essentials, but commitment is where the magic happens. Once you commit to doing something, really commit to it, you are on your way. And if you keep committing, you become unstoppable.

....

Our brain is now on a mission and will do whatever it needs to do to bring us a successful result. This will include making us aware of opportunities, bringing things of potential interest to our attention and suggesting things to do. It will also provide us with learning opportunities and give us insights, introduce us to the right people and make links between seemingly disparate things. When one route fails, it will suggest another. This is why commitment makes us unstoppable. Without it, you can dream as much you want and nothing will ever change.

How should I set my goals?

In whichever way works for you. It's easy for someone like me to set out a formula for you to follow, but life isn't like that and what works well for some people will leave others finding it confusing or simplistic, or even patronising, fussy or silly. If you *really* want to achieve something and you *genuinely* decide to do it then you will do it. So I won't give you any 'rules' but I will give you a few ideas you might want to build into your personal goal-setting.

SMART is a time-honoured and useful discipline widely used in business. Let's be strictly honest, it's widely known but often ignored, to the detriment of clarity and achievement. It stands for Specific, Measurable, Achievable, Relevant and Timed. I don't propose to do a mini session on this here as information on it is widely available, but I would like to pick out a few elements that I feel will make a huge difference to your ability to translate an idea into something tangible.

Measuring achievement can be hard to do, especially for a personal goal. So how do you know when you've achieved something worthwhile, or whether you're on track for making that achievement? These are important questions. We know how easily we are distracted, how quickly we become despondent, and how emotional we can be when it comes to judging ourselves and others.

This is where it helps to include some form of measurement in our plans so that we can review progress through facts rather than feelings. You will get feedback in the form of feelings anyway, hopefully including the pleasure and increasing feeling of control over your life that comes with success, but without empirical evidence you can be tempted to fall back on old patterns of thinking and behaviour. Such patterns could cause you to slow down or give up altogether, based on nothing but assumption. Set some measures as part of your plan from the beginning, including some stepping stones, as well as the final goal.

To be successful it is good to know right from the beginning what that success will look like, otherwise you could lose sight of what you're aiming for. Being able to tick things off on the way to your ultimate goal is not only emotionally rewarding but practical too, as one thing leads to another and each 'win' reinforces our feelings of progress and control.

Relevant to whom? When you come to set your goal it is worth thinking about who you are doing it for. There are so many directions we could possibly go in and so many fields we can plan to conquer that we need to be sure we are aiming for the one we want to conquer most. We can have many goals, but we can only truly focus on one at any given time. What do you really want to do so much that you would like, I should say *love*, to get started right now?

. . . .

'It's no good running a pig farm badly for 30 years while saying, 'Really, I was meant to be a ballet dancer.' By then, pigs will be your style.' English writer and raconteur Quentin Crisp

. . . .

There are goals that other people tell you to do and there are those that others want you to do. You are not living your life to achieve someone else's dreams, no matter how much you may love or admire them, you are here to achieve your own. There is no point in achieving something if achieving it won't make you happy and being skilled at something doesn't mean that you should keep on doing it – what if you could be even more skilled at something else and enjoy it more?

Time and energy are at a premium and we don't want to waste them doing things we have no interest in doing. Also, we don't want to waste them by doing nothing very much and not being happy about it. Indeed the more time you spend on something that has meaning for you, the better you will feel. The more you enjoy something, the more you will want to do it.

A goal doesn't have to be big. It might seem modest to anyone other than you, but it must be significant. It could be stopping biting your fingernails or getting a new job; it could be walking into a room without feeling self-conscious or setting up your own small business. If it means something to you, then that's your goal. When you achieve it, celebrate – and then set another one.

Time. Without a deadline or timescale your goal is just a dream. You need something to provide that little bit of tension that will kick your brain into gear and get it working on your goal. If you don't set these parameters it is difficult to keep momentum and easy to put things off. Another thing time helps with is accountability, firstly for yourself because it makes your choice clear – you can ask yourself if you are really going to make this happen or are you just playing at it. Do you want it enough to meet your own deadline? You'll get your answer soon enough.

There's another aspect to achievement that I haven't touched on yet because although it affects you profoundly, it's not directly about you. Your goal may depend on other people as well as you, and you may feel frustrated because they promise to do things and end up not doing them, or do them so slowly or half-heartedly that they might as well not have bothered. Deadlines help here as well. You can't hold someone to a deadline in the same way you can hold yourself, but you can use deadlines to demonstrate to you whether your friend or colleague is worth persevering with. If not, then you will need to find someone else, or find a way to do it on your own.

Waiting for someone who has made a promise they don't mean or expecting someone to care as much about your goal as you do can derail you, reinforcing the difficulties you face and providing further proof of failure. Sometimes you have to kiss a few frogs (rather than eat them this time!) before you find a prince and, again, it's best to kiss them quick until you find the one who will help turn your dream into reality.

I have a dream

Dreams are great! I have scored hat-tricks at Wembley and taken six wickets in an over, made word-perfect speeches, dated film stars and run rings around my opponents in debates. Some of those things are even possible, and one or two I have, in fact, experienced in reality. But there are some things I have to accept that I will never do.

I will never open the bowling for England. I'm way too old and I didn't put the practice in when I was young enough to. Plus, I didn't have the talent. Having said that, I did take six wickets in an over once. Against poor opposition. In twilight. With a chair for a wicket. So that little dream needs to be set to one side and stay as a dream where it's perfectly harmless.

Some people try to use that kind of unfulfilled dream as evidence that setting goals and working towards them is worthless. They claim that because you cannot achieve the impossible it is somehow dishonest to encourage people to dream big. This is disingenuous, and often put forward by those who have no intention of doing the work necessary to achieve their desire. Like the boy in Chapter One who claimed he wanted to be an astronaut (see also page 19), I never seriously entertained the idea of being a professional cricketer, and therefore I never seriously did any of the work that would give me the possibility of ever becoming one.

Does that prove there is no point in setting goals with focus, passion and belief, and committing to achieving them? No, it proves the exact opposite. Dreams can turn into reality, but only if you let them.

Dreams, Goals and Targets:
What's the Difference – And Does It Matter?
Takeaways from Chapter Nine

★ The very fact of creating goals for yourself increases your chances of success compared to those who don't set them at all

★ **If you are content with where you are, you don't need to do anything different. Just enjoy it and appreciate the people who share it with you**

★ If you are not happy with one or more aspects of your life, feeling sorry for yourself is not a permanent solution, and having a goal to aim for will be enormously helpful

★ **Whatever your goal, you need to want it with passion; there has to be pleasure in it, enjoyment, fun, triumph, victory over yourself, your fears, perceived adversity, whatever it is that means something to you.** Nothing **beats setting yourself a challenging goal, even one that you or others assumed was impossible, and achieving it**

★ If you don't believe you can do something, you won't do it

★ **Focus, passion and belief are essentials, but commitment is where the magic happens. Once you commit to doing something,** really **commit to it, you are on your way. And if you keep committing, you become unstoppable!**

CHAPTER TEN

Staying Out of Your Own Way

This has been quite a journey and at various points along the way it will have made you acknowledge behaviours and beliefs you might prefer not to face. That's not only a good thing, but an essential one. By this point in your journey you will know that in accepting your reality you are making the first step towards dealing with it and, where necessary, changing it.

If we deny our issues, we can never resolve them. This is how evolution works: the species that adapt most successfully to their challenges are the ones that survive. Your evolution is no different as the challenges you face *and overcome* are those that provide you with the skills you need to adapt, survive and succeed. That's a great start, but evolution is a continuous process and we know that as soon as we meet one challenge, there is another one coming up behind it. Flash-in-the-pan successes are no good to us. Having learned how to get out of our own way once, we now need to equip ourselves with some permanent skills, attitudes and techniques that will help us to *stay* out of our own way in the future. You've done it once, now you need to be able to do it again, and again. And enjoy doing it. That's what this chapter is about.

Houston, we have a problem

Would you like to be told you've got a problem? Your answer will depend on a lot of things, including the nature of the problem, the circumstances, the seriousness of the problem, including possible implications of success or failure, and your current state of mind. Mostly, we associate problems with bad things: something is stopping us, getting in our way or making things difficult. We typically respond to problems by worrying about them and in so doing we often make them worse, adding some new problems of our own in the form of doubt, hesitation and avoidance.

We need to learn to see a problem as an opportunity. Easy to say, I know, but much more difficult to do – until you think about all the people who thrive on having problems and resolving them. A problem is an opportunity: it's a chance to remove an obstacle, to come up with a better alternative than we currently have. It's an opportunity to get involved, be creative and make a change. Worry doesn't solve problems, ideas do. Think evolution and the species that survive through adapting to circumstances, facing life-threatening conditions and coming up with life-changing solutions.

All sorts of people welcome problems because of the advantages they give them. Sounds unrealistic? Scientific research is predicated on actively seeking problems and testing your solutions to destruction; theatre directors take on 'difficult' plays and staging problems because of the opportunity it gives them to achieve something remarkable.

· ·

Worry doesn't solve problems, ideas do.

· ·

Chris Hadfield in the book *An Astronaut's Guide To Life On Earth*, explains his own take on the role of problem-solving that neatly sums up what I'm saying and adds an extra element to it. Hadfield is the American astronaut who in 2013 sang Bowie's 'Space Oddity' in earth orbit on the international space station. He describes his NASA training regime as a series of simulations in which his trainers would come up with as many ways as they could think of to kill him.

The purpose of the training was to make him an expert in problem solving, including anticipating problems and preventing them, so after each session he left having ticked off one more solution to one more possible disaster. He says in his book: 'Like most astronauts, I'm pretty sure that I can deal with what life throws at me because I've thought about what to do if things go wrong, as well as right. That's the power of negative thinking.'

A problem does not mean it's the end of the world. It could well be the first step towards the next stage in your plan to conquer the world, or your industry, or even yourself. In solving a problem we are challenged to be better than we were: more creative, more resilient, more disciplined, less worried, less hesitant. We can solve a problem in any number of ways, but if we had no problems at all then we would have nothing driving us on to improve.

It's the same with stress: we are used to seeing stress as a bad thing, and of course it can be a very bad thing. But try to imagine a life with no stress at all, one with no sense of urgency and no need to get anything done, no challenges to inspire us, no goals to motivate us, no problems to solve, no need to improve anything. It may superficially seem like a nice idea when you're feeling stressed by the demands of your life as it is now but with no stress at all why would you even bother to get up in the morning?

....

Try to stop viewing problems as bad news and consider them as opportunities. The more problems you face, the more you can solve, and each problem solved takes you closer to achieving the outcome you are looking for.

....

A problem is a situation requiring action. That's it. It won't always be easy but at least the concept is simple! If something isn't the way you would like it to be, change something. It may be that you can change the situation or it may be you can't, but you can change your attitude towards it, or find the elements you can change and work on them, such as how you relate to the people around you or taking action to develop your skill set so you build your ability to take the action required.

....

'There is no such thing as a problem without a gift for you in its hands. You seek problems because you need their gifts.' Richard Bach, author of Illusions: The Adventures of a Reluctant Messiah

....

In order to stay out of your own way you need to (within reason) stop viewing problems as bad news and consider them opportunities. The more problems you face, the more you can solve, and each problem solved takes you a step closer to achieving the outcome you are looking for.

Resilience

Resilience is the ability to cope with whatever life throws at you and keep on going. Building your resilience is a prerequisite for everything we have discussed throughout this book. Without it you will be tempted to give up on your dream at the first sign of a problem. Here are a few useful ways of looking at resilience and the impact it has on our ability to lead a productive and fulfilling life.

In his seminal book *The Road Less Travelled*, M. Scott Peck talks about the difference between instant and deferred gratification. Writing in 1978, Peck's analysis holds up well today and provides insight into a range of current societal and individual problems. He identified a key difference between those who seek instant gratification and those who are prepared to work hard, take responsibility and understand that true satisfaction comes from having done something to achieve it.

Those who want things now, without the requirement to plan, prepare and work to get it, can at worst become intellectually and emotionally lazy and take less pleasure in what they have than those who work for them. Unfulfilled, they then move on to the next thing they want, and the next, without valuing what they already have. I believe that the growth of credit and the collective change in attitude towards borrowing directly led to the credit crunch and recession from 2010 onwards. If you earn money and immediately pay it out to credit companies there is no pleasure in earning it; you have no freedom of choice about what to do with your cash because it isn't really yours. That shiny new piece of equipment in your lounge or parked in your drive isn't really yours either because you haven't earned it.

. . . .

Giving up is easy. Keeping going is tough. Both statements are true in the short term, but false in the long term.

. . . .

If you see pleasure and fulfilment as a right, rather than something to be earned, you are setting yourself up for disappointment. Having them fails to satisfy you and not having them makes you resentful. It's not all about the journey, as many try to tell you, but the journey itself is an essential step towards arriving.

'The truth is that our finest moments are most likely to occur when we are feeling deeply uncomfortable, unhappy, or unfulfilled. For it is only in such moments, propelled by our discomfort, that we are likely to step out of our ruts and start searching for different ways or truer answers.' M. Scott Peck, author of The Road Less Travelled

We can't know for certain what the end of the journey will be when we start it, but if we don't have something to aim for then we will not even know which direction to travel in. Once we start travelling we need to keep going, even if we have to change course every now and again or stop temporarily to take stock or overcome the roadblocks in our way. We may need to revise our destination slightly, or change the way we are travelling, but as long as we are moving forwards then we will keep on learning, keep on improving and keep on achieving. Keep in your head the reasons you set off on the road in the first place, and if those reasons are still relevant to you then the journey is still worthwhile.

Giving up is easy. Keeping going is tough. Both statements are true in the short term, but false in the long term.

Being organised is one way of maintaining our resilience. While we are used to organising ourselves at work and following procedures, we are not used to doing so in our personal lives. I have to say that the prospect of organising myself outside of work doesn't appeal to me but there is a case for introducing an element of organisation into our lives.

It can be difficult to keep doing the right things if you don't know what those things are. Being organised ensures that you have at least thought about what you should be doing and when, and that gives you a fighting chance of being able to do it. but it doesn't have to be anything complex or time-consuming, in fact, the simpler the better. Here are a few truths I've found out for myself:

- If I want to be spontaneous, I have to be organised first. The reason for this is that if I want to be able to take advantage of an opportunity to do something then I have to be in a position to do so. I need to have the time to do it, which I won't have if I'm behind with everything and up against deadlines of my own making. I need to have the resources to do it, so if, for example, it costs money then I need to have managed my finances well enough to be able to afford the random expenditure involved. I need to have the energy to do it, which I won't have if I've worn myself out worrying or working too hard on the wrong things

- If I start something without having done at least some rudimentary planning, I am far more likely to abandon it because I get ambushed by something I hadn't prepared for. I might not have allowed myself the time to understand the task I am trying to complete. I might understand it myself but not have given any partners or colleagues the time to understand

their roles, and I might not have taken the time to understand
their perspective

- If I don't have a plan, I have no idea whether what I am doing
will make any difference. I could be wasting my time on
something peripheral when I would be better off doing
something else entirely, or even nothing at all.

Keeping things simple is a good idea. The more complex
something becomes, the less enthused I will be about doing it. We
can keep things simple by 'chunking' our bigger tasks into a series
of smaller ones, then we can feel good for having dealt with each of
them in turn. I'm sure you will have had the experience of being
overwhelmed by the sheer volume of things you have to do, and
the feeling that you simply cannot do it all. Our instinctive
response is to run away from it, putting it off until another day
that may not ever come.

Completing a big project or working towards an overall 'aim'
makes it harder to keep going than if you identify a set of actions
to take that can be done in one 'bite', such as booking some lessons
or arranging to meet a specific person. Don't set yourself up to fail,
set yourself up to succeed. Be pleased with what you've done and
move on to the next thing – they add up to something significant.

Your habits become your life

In the end it all comes down to this: your habits become your life.
How you habitually think leads directly to what you habitually do.

Most of our decisions are not decisions at all, they are the expression of our habitual thoughts and behaviours.

····························

Your habits become your life. Most of our decisions are not decisions at all, they are the expression of our habitual thoughts and behaviours.

····························

Changing habits is not something we can generally achieve through sheer force of will. We will not change them simply by saying we will, and attempting to cling on for dear life to our new way of thinking and behaving. As we saw in Chapters Two and Three (pages 25 and 41), and indeed throughout this book, we are up against a formidable opponent: our subconscious. If we try to fight our subconscious in a battle of wills there can only be one winner. It's a complicated dance between our conscious mind, which may want to change how we see the world, and our subconscious that is trying to protect us by clinging to all the old messages we have given it in the past. It seeks to protect us and keep us safe; that's all it wants to do, and it tries to do that by carrying out all our well-established instructions.

To our subconscious mind the old, tried-and-tested ways are good, new and untested is bad. This is why New Year's resolutions are traditionally pointless. Resolutions are about big gestures – and big gestures are hard work. Given that hard work is, well, hard, our brains are more than happy to come up with counterarguments to prove that what we have resolved to do is a really bad idea. The set-piece resolution is meat and drink to our subconscious. It's typically so big, so ambitious and so absolute that your brain can easily dismiss it in favour of something safer and vaguely reassuring. What your brain is doing is keeping you in your (often uncomfortable) comfort zone. It does this by justifying the old habit and preventing you from trying to build a new one.

It's not the big gestures that make the difference, it's the regular dripfeed of smaller, less dramatic interventions that gives us the best chance of helping our subconscious to understand and accept our new thinking.

My daughter holds the family record for broken resolutions for declaring as the chimes started that she would stop cracking her knuckles, only to crack them again before the chimes had finished. Why did she do that? Because cracking her knuckles was a habit. The Oxford English Dictionary defines a habit as a '*settled or regular tendency or practice, especially one that is hard to give up*'. This applies to working long hours, not listening properly or, indeed, cracking your knuckles. Something as ingrained in us as that won't be turned around simply because we make an announcement.

The OED also defines a habit as '*an automatic reaction to a specific situation*', a definition that takes us even deeper into our subconscious. A habit is not just ingrained behaviour, it is an automatic response to a given situation. This means that every time we face a similar situation we *react in the same way*. So, we're doomed (Private Fraser's stock response in the BBC comedy series *Dad's Army*). Fraser saw disaster as the inevitable result of any problem; in the same way, we all jump immediately to our own stock responses.

We saw earlier that, faced with an important deadline, the perfectionists among us may well obsess about small details, not acting until everything is perfectly in place. Our dithering means we leave everything until the last minute and end up rushing, or missing out altogether. Either way, the result is imperfection and missed opportunity – the very things we were desperate to avoid.

If we are impulsive, we do the opposite – diving in and making mistakes because we simply didn't stop long enough to plan and prepare. We end up taking on too much, over-complicating things and making mistakes that take longer to sort out than they would have done to prevent in the first place. This leads to more unproductive work, more discouragement and perhaps abandoning as too much trouble something we were originally excited about. So often we end up causing the very thing we are trying to avoid. What's that all about? How difficult can it be to do what we want to do?

Many of us go about change in the wrong way, giving our subconscious a great excuse to stop us changing. Get up at 6 a.m.

and go for a run, or lie in, where it's warm and comfortable? No contest! Trust someone else to do something you've always done, or keep doing it yourself? Easy! A few days of running and your brain (OK, and your body too) will tell you what a good effort you've made and isn't it time you had a rest? Diets generally don't work because we still associate pleasure with eating and pain with not eating. Think of the offices where people sit around talking about diets only to join in the next bun round – the new habit has no chance to get established.

Only you can overcome this, and the only way is to associate pain with continuing with the old negative habit and pleasure with establishing a new positive one. In doing so, we need to work with our subconscious and not against it. We must avoid putting ourselves on guard against the new thinking otherwise our brains will protect us against the new dangers and defend the status quo that we've been 'happy' with up to now. Absolutes won't work (I'm going to stop wasting time, I will be more decisive), desirable results are a more realistic focus than wishes (I will be able to take my dream holiday or I will run a half-marathon by the end of the year). We need to reinforce the benefits of the new to prevent the old from seeming more sensible.

Consistency is a good thing to aim for if you are serious about staying out of your own way. You know all the old habits and all the counterproductive behaviours and how easy it is to fall back into them. The usual rules apply though; don't beat yourself up if you slip back into old habits. When you do (and, inevitably, you will from time to time) just acknowledge it, work out why, and start again. The more consistently you apply any of the techniques in this book, plus any you find elsewhere that work for you, the easier it will become.

The power of affirmation

In order to imbed our new, positive internal messages into our subconscious, we need to somehow out-talk the old stuff. We don't want our brain to spend its time thinking about the old, negative stuff anymore. The instructions that tell us what we can't do, don't believe and will never have are no good to us now, and never were: we just got used to them.

Bearing in mind that these messages became ingrained in us over a period of years and even decades, out-talking them might seem like a long and impossible task. However, while estimates vary, it is generally believed that we can successfully out-talk our old habits and replace them with new ones in a matter of weeks rather than years.

One of the most powerful methods of doing this is the affirmation. An affirmation is a positive statement, describing yourself as having already achieved the state you are aiming for. While it is easy to make fun of someone for apparently claiming to be, for example, wealthy and influential when they are patently neither of those things, it is a surprisingly effective technique.

....

Affirmations are a way of giving your brain a new set of instructions. All you need to do is repeat those instructions often enough for your brain to realise that you mean it. It will then seek to act in accordance with those instructions. Change can then follow because you are allowing it to.

....

Our negative self-talk, as described in Chapter Three (page 41), can be described as a lie. We can say this because our self-talk tends to be absolute, leaving no room for doubt or contradiction as we describe ourselves as 'always' this or 'never' that. Whether we are describing ourselves as big fat ugly monsters, people with nothing interesting to say, or as shy or stupid or unlucky, we seem to be pretty confident about it! We therefore believe that lie.

If we work on these negative assessments of ourselves, or of the world in general, we are working on the core beliefs that are holding us back. It makes no logical sense but what we are doing is instructing our subconscious to make those things come true, and if we believe they are true then there is literally no point in trying to disprove them. That's how absolutes work: they are absolute. So why not replace those absolutes with a different absolute that happens to be positive?

If we take the examples I listed earlier in this chapter, we can see the effect on our outlook and the prospects of changing those negative lies to positive ones. If instead of seeing herself as a 'fat ugly hideous monster', the young woman I discussed in Chapter Three (page 41) started describing herself as 'slim, kind, clever and attractive', what difference would it make to her behaviour? At first, she would see this description as ridiculous and wrong, but if repeated often enough to out-talk her previous lie, what would her brain need to do?

In order to integrate this new way of seeing herself, her brain would start to adjust her mental picture of herself, which would create tension between what she currently thinks she is, and what her new affirmation now says she is. It would work to resolve that tension, and one of the things it would enable her to do would be to welcome the help and support on offer and open her eyes to the opportunities for change in lifestyle and outlook: change your self-talk and you begin to influence the choices you make. Her affirmation would now be: 'I am slim, kind, clever and attractive'. I'm not saying this is what everyone should aim to be, I'm using it as an example of how she could, if she were willing, change her destructive self-image and her counterproductive behaviour associated with it.

If you tell yourself you have nothing interesting to say, and you have told yourself that for years, you will probably end up not saying very much. If, however, you tell yourself instead that you have much to contribute that is worthwhile and interesting then you will feel more like sharing it with others. Equally, if you say you are confident (instead of saying you are shy) or lucky (instead of unlucky), you will start to behave according to your new pack of lies instead of your old ones.

You are giving your brain a new set of instructions. All you need to do is repeat those instructions often enough for your brain to realise that you mean it. It will then seek to act in accordance with those instructions. Change can then follow because you are allowing it to.

Here are a few things to consider if you are planning to use affirmations. The American self-help speaker and writer Jack Canfield is a useful man to go to here:

Use the present tense rather than the future. An affirmation works best if you are setting up some tension between where you are now and where you want to be. If you are merely stating a wish or hope, or saying you might get there some day, there is no stress to be resolved and therefore no pressure to act. Once your brain realises that you are claiming to already have arrived and are already in a different place, it will redouble its efforts to try to get you there.

....

Your affirmation is like a satnav: give it a vague instruction and you will arrive somewhere in the vicinity, give it a specific address and it will take you exactly where you want to go.

....

Second that emotion. Include some words that convey to you how important this is to you. Above all, show yourself how much you will enjoy the experience of getting there and arriving. Use words like 'love', 'enjoy' and 'passion' even if those words make you feel just a little uncomfortable to start with.

Be as specific as you can in describing what you want your new state to be. Your affirmation is like a satnav: give it a vague instruction and you will arrive somewhere in the vicinity, give it a specific address and it will take you straight to the doorstep. Satnavs are great – they don't criticise you for your wrong turns, they offer alternative routes and they follow your instructions. The more accurate your instructions, the more useful the feedback.

Here are a few ideas for affirmations based on the examples I gave earlier:

• •

'I love being slim, kind, clever and attractive.'

'I enjoy having interesting conversations with people I meet.'

'People really appreciate what I have to say and I enjoy listening to them.'

'I am a lucky person. I have everything I need.'

• •

Yes, these are all lies, to begin with.

Visualisation

Visualisation is another great technique for reinforcing the outcome you are heading towards. It achieves in pictures what an affirmation achieves in words. If you are a visual person then having an image of your ideal destination somewhere you can see it every day is a powerful way of keeping it to the front of your mind. It may be a picture of you at the door of the house you want your family to live in, a quote that inspires you, a cheque in full payment of your mortgage, a venue you want to perform at or a skill you would like to possess. As long as it conveys the satisfaction you will gain from achieving the goal along with the passion, the belief and the commitment that will bring it to you, it can provide you with the motivation to keep working towards your target.

Over to you!

There's a (very) old series of jokes, one of which goes: 'How many psychologists does it take to change a light bulb? Answer: One. But the light bulb has to really want to change'. This book is there for you if there are aspects of your life you want to change for the better. I hope there have been a few true 'light bulb' moments for you along the way and that you feel empowered to get out of your own way and work towards your own personal ambitions.

One final thought: Harry Potter discovers the Mirror of Erised ('Desire' spelt backwards) – a mirror that shows you 'nothing other than your heart's desire'. Professor Dumbledore tells Harry that the happiest man on earth would look in the mirror and see himself exactly as he is, while others have wasted away their entire lives staring into the mirror, unable to tear themselves away from their vision of the perfect life.

I said in the introduction to this book that the biggest influence on your life for good or ill is the person looking back at you from your own mirror each morning. The man or woman in the mirror is the only person who can make the changes you need or want to make. That person can help you to have, if not the 'perfect' life promised by so many self-help gurus, then an infinitely better one than you have allowed yourself in the past. As you look in the mirror now, I hope that person looks different from when you started reading this book.

The only person who can hold you back is you. Similarly, the only person who can take you forward is you. As you reach the end of this book I hope you have come to know yourself better, and have picked up some tools to enable you to take control of your own life. Stop doing the things that hold you back and start doing the things that will take you where you want to be. Stop worrying and start thinking; stop looking for excuses and look instead for the next opportunity; stop blaming yourself for past mistakes and learn from them instead. It's time to look forward and enjoy life. It's time to get out (and stay out) of your own way.

Staying Out of Your Own Way:
Takeaways from Chapter Ten

★ Worry doesn't solve problems, ideas do

★ **Try to stop viewing problems as bad news and consider them as opportunities. The more problems you face, the more you can solve, and each problem solved takes you closer to achieving the outcome you are looking for**

★ Giving up is easy. Keeping going is tough. Both statements are true in the short term, but false in the long term

★ **Your habits become your life. Most of our decisions are not decisions at all, they are the expression of our habitual thoughts and behaviours**

★ Affirmations are a way of giving your brain a new set of instructions. All you need to do is repeat those instructions often enough for your brain to realise that you mean it. It will then seek to act in accordance with those instructions. Change can then follow because you are allowing it to

★ **Your affirmation is like a satnav: give it a vague instruction and you will arrive somewhere in the vicinity, give it a specific address and it will take you exactly where you want to go**

★ Get out (and stay out) of your own way.

BIBLIOGRAPHY

Allen, David, *Getting Things Done* (Piatkus, 2001).

Bach, Richard, *Jonathan Livingston Seagull: A Story* (Harper Thorsons, 2015).

Canfeld, Jack, *The Success Principles: How to Get From Where You Are to Where You Want to Be* (Element, 2005).

Carnegie, Dale, *How to Stop Worrying and Start Living* (Vermilion, 1998).

Collins, Jim, *Good To Great: Why Some Companies Make the Leap and Others Don't* (Random House, 2001).

Covey, Stephen R., *7 Habits of Highly Effective People: Powerful Lessons in Personal Change* (DC Books, 2005).

Frankl, Victor E., *Man's Search for Meaning* (Rider, 2004).

Gladwell, Malcolm, *Outliers: The Story of Success* (Penguin, 2009).

Gladwell, Malcolm *Blink: The Power of Thinking Without Thinking* (Penguin, 2006).

Hadfield, Chris, *An Astronaut's Guide to Life on Earth* (Macmillan, 2013).

Hester, Alan, *Management Starts With You* (Robinson, 2017).

Jeffers, Susan, *Feel the Fear And Do It Anyway: How to Turn Your Fear and Indecision into Confidence and Action* (Vermilion, 2007).

Kimmage, Paul, *Full Time: The Secret Life of Tony Cascarino* (Simon & Schuster, 2005).

Scott Peck, M., *The Road Less Travelled* (Arrow, 1990).

Springsteen, Bruce, *Born To Run* (Simon & Schuster, 2016).

Tracy, Brian, *Eat That Frog! Get More of the Important Things Done Today* (Hodder, 2013).

Turner, Colin, *Born to Succeed* (Texere, 2002).

INDEX